WALK IN
GENERATIONAL
BLESSINGS

LEAVING A LEGACY OF TRANSFORMATION
THROUGH YOUR FAMILY

JOSEPH MATTERA

DESTINY IMAGE® PUBLISHERS, INC.

P.O. Box 310, Shippensburg, PA 17257-0310

"Promoting Inspired Lives."

This book and all other Destiny Image, Revival Press, MercyPlace, Fresh Bread, Destiny Image Fiction, and Treasure House books are available at Christian bookstores and distributors worldwide.

For a U.S. bookstore nearest you, call **1-800-722-6774.**

For more information on foreign distributors, call **717-532-3040.**

Reach us on the Internet: **www.destinyimage.com.**

ISBN 13 TP: 978-0-7684-4060-7

ISBN 13 Ebook: 978-0-7684-8892-0

For Worldwide Distribution, Printed in the U.S.A.

1 2 3 4 5 6 7 8 / 16 15 14 13 12

ENDORSEMENTS

Humans did not lose Heaven in the Garden of Eden as a result of the Fall. Rather, humans lost dominion as God had intended for them in His original plan. Heaven as we know it is regained through receiving Jesus Christ as our personal Savior and Lord—it is 100 percent due to His efficacious sacrifice and not due to anything on our part. However, as Dr. Joseph Mattera explains and encourages in *Walk in Generational Blessings*, the lost dominion is regained by us following biblical mandates and principles that are futuring, process-driven, and ultimately transgenerational. To say this book is challenging would be an understatement. To say it is transformational would be accurate. Read this book and begin a transgenerational transformational journey.

Dr. Samuel R. Chand
Author, *Cracking Your Church's Culture Code*
www.samchand.com

Do not mistake this volume for a simple view of the problems of our planet. Joseph Mattera has taken the subject in hand and has plunged into the heart of the matter that lies beneath the surface of this troubled world. His position is more than just a simple result of a proper worldview. It is nearer to a cosmic view, if you please, a view from the very throne of

God. Isn't it time that we took a view of the realities of our planet from the perspective of the Kingdom of God, the realm of God's rule?

This is precisely what Joseph Mattera has dared to do. He confronts political correctness and pluralism head-on, boldly declaring that what God told us to begin with is still true today. He has identified a cultural mandate to consider a biblical worldview and its implications and dares to tell us that this is the only answer to our seemingly complex dilemma.

The answer is "hidden in plain sight" in the family structure, the original plan of God, and a return to the sanctity of marriage. Herein is the only formula for recovery of the soul of the world. Stopping cultural decline cannot be accomplished in the halls of government or in the laboratories of science and technology or on the battlefields of clashing cultures, but in the heart of our society—the home.

Joseph tears away the veneer of what has been deemed culturally acceptable and exposes the fallacies that are seeking to rip to shreds our ancient and long-cherished values. As an example, he dares to expose abortion as "genocide in slow motion."

This book should be read deliberately, thoughtfully, and thoroughly, with the reader taking copious notes as our first contribution toward a cure to the sickness into which our culture is sinking. The approach is solidly biblical and thoroughly practical and clearly instructs how what we have lost may be recovered.

It engages the pressing questions, "Have we gone too far?" "Can we recover?" "Where do we start with the solution?" With all the ominous alarms that are sounded, it is a book of overwhelming hope and crystal clear strategy. It deserves our attention and demands a response from all of us.

Jack Taylor
Dimensions Ministries
Melbourne, Florida

I wish I had written this awesome, biblical presentation on generational blessing. Bishop Mattera has crafted a book for parents and grandparents who want to be in a position to leave a legacy of physical, relational, and spiritual blessings for their seed and seed's seed. Every Christian parent of any age, as well as their children, must read this!

Dr. Larry Keefauver
Best-selling author, international speaker, and teacher

Bishop Joseph Mattera has done it again. His book dares to challenge the status quo of this troubled nation. Our nation is in crisis, and Dr. Mattera goes straight to the heart of what's troubling our country. As many in the church community are combating attacks against the sanctity of life, marriage, and family, his book details the problems and gives us God's solutions to our issues. This book *Walk in Generational Blessings* helps us regain the Kingdom dominion given to humanity by God in the Garden of Eden. This is a must-read for any Kingdom-minded believer who desires to know the heart of God.

Bishop Eugene Reeves

So God created man in His own image; in the image of God He created him; male and female He created them. Then God blessed them, and God said to them, "Be fruitful and multiply; fill the earth and subdue it; have dominion over the fish of the sea, over the birds of the air, and over every living thing that moves on the earth" (Genesis 1:27-28 NKJV).

CONTENTS

FOREWORD

I was supposed to be in my 8th NBA season by now. Dropping long-range three pointers from the arc, shaking and baking with the basketball, leaving defenders off balance and embarrassed. That was the dream that was played over and over in my head for years. But the good Lord had something else in mind, and with me standing tall at only 5'10" and unable to jump to high heaven, well, I can't really blame Him. Don't get me wrong now—I was one excellent baller. I played with some of the best competition New York City had to offer, and was even fortunate enough to represent my city officially against other powerhouse teams from around the country.

Flash-forward to today.

I'm now the editor of one of the biggest conservative publications in the country, *Human Events*, a *New York Times* best-selling author, and a host on New York's flagship radio station, 77 WABC. I say that not to brag. Not at all. Rather, I mention that to say that such divergent career goals from when I was pursuing a professional sports career to where I am today as an author and activist could be pretty confusing for any young adult.

I, for one, was perplexed at the time.

"God, you want me to do what? Politics? But I'm not some egghead dork who goes on dates wearing a tweed jacket and watches C-SPAN all day!"

And I'm still not.

Yet the transition was nearly seamless, jumping through door after door God opened for me because of what you're about to read in my dad's book, *Walk in Generational Blessings*.

Joe Mattera can speak with authority about how to raise up children to be agents of influence, to attack life with God's purpose, and to serve as models for other families because he's lived it. I've seen it firsthand. And while it may seem like a rote platitude, the whole "make sure your kids serve God" thing, ask yourself this: How many ministers' children go astray, publicly humiliating and defying their church, their God, and their family? You've witnessed it. I've witnessed it.

It's sad actually. The number of young people today who were once ensconced in the Gospel only to turn their backs on their faith later on is one of the spectacular failures of modern Christianity. Newly minted adults are not prepared to live Christian lives amid work, hobbies, friendships, recreation, and relationships. Sure, they know Christian principles theoretically. But they fall short experientially.

The pages herewith are a blueprint on how to affect change presently and generationally: through family. We hear plenty of sermonizing regarding revivals, and of all-night prayer meetings, and of street evangelism, and of long fasts—which all have their proper place. But these important aspects of Christianity, without parental involvement and discipleship, often will not produce the desired results of building character, molding discipline, and setting a young person on a steady, unshakable Christian path. What does produce these desired results—the years of devotion parents spend with their children, constantly training them up in how to live orderly and God-centered lives. It's part of the family structure; it's the household DNA. To that family, it can be explained in one word: life.

I gave you two conclusions at the start of this Foreword. I told you what my plans were, but also what they ended up being. But I didn't give you the beginning and middle. The reason I was able to make a smooth shift from jock to pundit was the time my dad and mom spent instructing me as a kid and teenager.

When I was just barely able to talk, they both had me memorizing Bible verses. Before the age of 5 I was able to quote the Romans Road to Salvation, had almost the entire first chapter of the Gospel of John memorized, and knew each major Old and New Testament character. When I became a teenager and my passion for basketball really surged, Dad would drive me to basketball camps and used our trips as opportunities to teach me what it meant to have a biblical worldview—that is, to understand and appreciate how our faith informs our views on politics, government, the arts, the economy, and the like.

By the age of 16, I knew Christian apologetics backward and forward. Not because I was necessarily interested in this arena (I wasn't), but because Dad made it part of our father-son time.

So when it came time for me to defend Christian principles in class, I was ready. And good thing I was. You know the warnings you hear about young adults being lobotomized when they go off to college? All true. Conservative Christians are treated like second-class citizens on campus. Their ideas scorned and maligned. Think not? Just try walking down a nearby university's lecture hall with a Bible in one hand, the Constitution in the other, and rocking a shirt with Ronald Reagan's face emblazoned on it and see how fast you're brought before the university tribunal for inciting hate speech, you insensitive Jesus freak you!

Many times I was the only person in class challenging the professor's assumptions and biases. It was a blast. I absolutely loved it. And teachers feared it, which made me absolutely love it all the more. From there I went on to start my own newspaper, organized one of the biggest clubs on campus, and also hosted a controversial speaking series that required the school to book multiple overflow rooms to satisfy the demand of the student body who wanted to hear our message. (These events were labeled "controversial," mind you, because liberals couldn't stand hearing alternative viewpoints.)

I was entering the next season of my life, and was able to dive in without a hitch because of all the years prior that Mom and Dad spent preparing me, even though I didn't know it at the time.

I will always be grateful for that. I'm also grateful that Dad taught me how to fight. Fathers: every son needs to learn self-defense! And, for the record, there's nothing like jump-starting the fisticuff, testosterone-fueled sparring matches with a marathon of martial arts movies while Mom is away at a church women's retreat.

Of course, being properly equipped to defend the faith (and one's self) means nothing if you don't have a relationship with God. To this day, if I'm in a spiritual funk and tell my parents about it, their response is, "Have you prayed?" So true. Prayer is what lifts our souls and clears our minds. It takes our burden that we cannot bear and places it on Him who died to bear it in our stead. And those are not just words on a page to me. I've heard Mom and Dad implore their leaders similarly, heard them preach it from the pulpit, and, most importantly, heard them apply it to their own lives during challenging times. The Bible's enduring message of hope and confidence in Christ is real to me because I first saw it real for them.

Lastly, families need unbreakable bonds. They need to move together like a ship does. If part of the oar is broken, the ship will take longer to reach its destination. Likewise, if one part of the family unit is wobbly, it should concern everyone. That's how the Matteras have operated. We got each other's backs. A crisis for one is a crisis for all. We spend time together, not because we have to, but because we want to. Our love for each other is deep and manifest. So are our friendships. For me, I have the privilege of being the oldest of five children. Without hesitation, it's the title in life that I value the most. I'm the big brother. I'd choose that over every material possession I own.

And yet much of modern Christianity's message is individualistic. We relegate God to the role of cosmic sugar daddy. It's all about what He can do for us. But when you pore over the pages of this book, you'll realize that God sparks momentum, blessings, and legacy through the channels of family. That's worth repeating: the vehicle God uses to bring us to our destination is through our lineage.

God calls all of us to be leaders. How do I know? Because He's called us to be mothers and fathers, to protect and nurture the most important flock of all—our children.

You're a leader. Now go get reading, pilgrim.

Jason Mattera
Editor, *Human Events*
New York Times best-selling author

PREFACE

MANY years ago, my eyes were opened as to the importance of planning and thinking generationally in everything I do. Hence, *Walk in Generational Blessings* is the most important work I have ever written! It is my life message, as I carry the same kind of burden that was on Elijah the prophet when he was called to restore *"the hearts of the fathers to the children, and the hearts of the children to their fathers…"* (Mal. 4:6-7 NKJV). This work has come out of my many hours of studying the Scriptures, raising five biological children in the context of a Christian home and local church, and my observation that the Body of Christ by and large acts as though the Kingdom of God is merely one-generational, not multigenerational. I pray that the Lord will impart a vision in every reader's heart to participate in the generational plan of God as shown in the purpose statement God gave the human race in Genesis 1:28.

INTRODUCTION

THE goal I have for this book is twofold: to prove that the Bible teaches that salvation and cultural dominion is primarily accomplished generationally through families and to give practical steps that will empower parents and churches to release the next generation to fulfill their purpose in Christ. To accomplish this, we will work our way through a specialized biblical survey, carefully studying and analyzing data from the Old to the New Testament as it relates to God's plan for a multigenerational blessing through the family.

At the time of the writing of this book, my mother, Miriam Mattera, recently passed on to be with the Lord, and on the same day of her "homegoing" service, my youngest son, Justin, was leading our regular congregational Sunday services for Youth Day, which turned out to be some of the most powerful services we had in 2010! This was significant to me because my mother's mother, Antoinette, was the primary person responsible for leading my mother to Christ, and my mom was the primary person responsible for leading me to faith in Christ! When the youth took the lead on that particular Sunday, I couldn't help but think how significant it was that Justin was taking the lead on the day his grandmother was eulogized! It exemplified the incredible generational nature of the Kingdom of God like nothing else I have ever experienced!

As we neared the conclusion of 2010, I began to reflect on the condition of my homeland, the United States of America. Our nation is becoming more and more secular, with many organizations and chain stores trying to completely expunge Christ from Christmas. There is a raging battle over the definition of marriage; the "don't ask don't tell" policy that bans gays from the military has been lifted, while atheists are attacking the historical legitimacy of Jesus Christ and writing best-selling books.

I can remember like it was just yesterday when Judge Roy Moore lost his court case and was ordered to remove a monument depicting the biblical Ten Commandments from his Alabama courthouse. The three plaques with inspiration from the Psalms have been ordered removed from the South Rim of the Grand Canyon after being there for over 30 years. There is even talk of removing the Ten Commandments from the United States Supreme Court.

In spite of all this, I am filled with hope! You may think that as a Christian living in these unsettling times, I am crazy for still having a positive attitude. But as you read the following pages, I pray that you will clearly see the reason I have hope and what I believe is the single most important strategy found in the Bible for winning back our culture to Christ.

I have been personally involved with numerous city-wide events, many of which were for the purpose of revival and taking our city for Christ. I have participated in city and national gatherings for fasting and prayer involving thousands of people. Standing on the platform while world renowned leaders taught, preached, or prayed for revival, I would look out at these vast audiences and think, *Most of these dear saints believe that this one event is going to somehow change their city or nation!*

We have trained ourselves in the charismatic, evangelical world to think in terms of events. We think and act as though we serve the God of Abraham (representing one generation) instead of understanding that we serve the God of Abraham, Isaac, and Jacob (multiple generations)!

In most of these events, we attempt to "shoot at the moon with a bullet," putting all of our work, money, time, and effort into an event that we declare to masses of Christians "will change our city or our nation."

It's like we only have one strategy for our warfare—the glory cloud coming over our city and instantaneously saving millions of souls at once. If we were military generals at war, it would be like saying we have no plan for winning the war except the dropping of a nuclear bomb! Although I believe we should continue to pray for revival and for that glory cloud to fall on our cities, we also need to be establishing an intergenerational offensive against the enemy.

Besides, even if millions were saved in one day, it's likely that most pastors would have nervous breakdowns after two months because of the pressure of keeping up with all these masses of people coming into their services! Most churches couldn't even handle 200 new people added to their church, never mind thousands! The very things we pray in our prayers for revival lack biblical strategies to the extent that God cannot even answer them. Given the current state of things in the Church, including the lack of commitment and capable leadership, how would a church effectively shepherd a barrage of newly saved people?

Deuteronomy 7:22 speaks to this principle when God was giving Israel His strategy for conquering the land of Canaan.

> *And the Lord thy God will put out those nations before thee by little and little: thou mayest not consume them at once, lest the beasts of the field increase upon thee.*

God cannot give His people more than they are capable of managing!

Unfortunately, the most important strategy for subduing and having dominion on the earth is missing at most of the aforementioned citywide events. I cannot remember one of these great ministers praying, preaching, or even mentioning what I believe is the most important command we have in the Bible in terms of reaching cities and nations for Christ!

CHAPTER 1

THE MOST IMPORTANT PASSAGE IN THE BIBLE

Our starting points determine the what, the why, and how we build a thing. —Joseph Mattera

EVERYTHING we do in life is determined by our starting point or our presuppositions. Every contractor presumes there is a well-thought-out blueprint to refer to that clearly defines what he is to build and why. Architecturally speaking, there can be no "how to build" unless the architect knows "what and why" something is to be built. Biblically speaking, this means what we are looking for is what we will find when we read the Bible. If my Bible reading is motivated by a goal of trying to feel God's love, I will personalize every verse and impose this theme into every passage of Scripture I read.

Consequently, we need to begin our understanding of God's will for us based on His original plan, His blueprint. Otherwise we will get caught up in the "sub-plots" of Scripture and miss the meta-narrative of God, or the big picture God has for His people. Our goal then is to focus on God's ultimate goal, our redemption through the Cross of Christ and how He works His purposes on the earth through families from one generation to the next.

The word *generation* comes from the root word *generate*, which means to bring something into existence, usually through physical or chemical processes. A generation is the act or process of generating and is made up of a group of individuals having a common ancestor and constituting a single stage of descent. The average time interval of a generation for humans, the time between the birth of parents and the birth of their off-spring, is approximately 30 years. A *genealogy* is a study of ancestry, usually a recording or accounting of the descent of a family, a group, or a specific person from an ancestor or family line.

THE BOOK OF BEGINNINGS

Appropriately, we will begin in the Book of Genesis, which is the "book of beginnings." As a matter of fact, this book contains in "seed form" all the major concepts and doctrines of the Christian faith. The one verse that can possibly summarize the contents of the book would be Genesis 2:4.

> *These are the generations of the heavens and of the earth when they were created, in the day that the Lord God made the earth and the heavens.*

The Hebrew word for generations is *towlâdah, tolâdah* (to·led·aw) and occurs 39 times in the Old Testament of the Bible, 38 times as "generations" and once as "birth."[1] *Vine's Dictionary of the Bible* expands on the definition, adding "descendants, results, proceedings, generations, genealogies; an account of men and their descendants; a genealogical list of one's descendants; one's contemporaries; course of history (of creation, etc.) and begetting or account of heaven."

I have never heard anyone say this before, but I believe Genesis 1:26-28 is the most important of all Scripture passages.

And God said, Let Us make man in Our image, after Our likeness: and let them have dominion over the fish of the sea, and over the fowl of the air, and over the cattle, and over all the earth, and over every creeping thing that creepeth upon the earth. So God created man in His own image, in the image of God created He him; male and female created He them. And God blessed them, and God said unto them, be fruitful, and multiply, and replenish the earth, and subdue it: and have dominion over the fish of the sea, and over the fowl of the air, and over every living thing that moveth upon the earth (Genesis 1:26-28).

I am not saying this portion of Scripture is the only one we should know or that other passages aren't important. My reason for choosing Genesis 1:26-28 is because it is the "covenant of creation," which God made with all of humanity through Adam. This passage is the purpose statement for all human beings who were yet to be born. Without this passage, we cannot know the original intent God had for creating humankind and this planet. It serves as the cornerstone, the lynchpin, or as they say in philosophy, the ontological and metaphysical reason for our very existence as humans!

Understanding this uncovers not only why we were born, but what we are supposed to do. Certain theologians call this passage of Scripture the cultural mandate because in it, Adam is given the express command to infect all of planet Earth with the knowledge and presence of God. Without understanding this, we can't even understand why the Lord Jesus came to planet Earth!

Truly, it is no coincidence that Jesus is called the Last (or Second) Adam in First Corinthians 15:45. In this verse, God ties the coming of Christ with Adam. Jesus came as the Second Adam to complete the work the first Adam did not finish when God gave him the original covenant of creation and his Cultural Commission. Romans 5:12-21 clearly shows that the mission of Jesus is inexorably connected to the first Adam.

Wherefore, as by one man sin entered into the world, and death by sin; and so death passed upon all men, for that all have sinned: (For until the law sin was in the world: but sin is not imputed when there is no law. Nevertheless death reigned from Adam to Moses, even over them that had not sinned after the similitude of Adam's transgression, who is the figure of Him that was to come. But not as the offence, so also is the free gift. For if through the offence of one many be dead, much more the grace of God, and the gift by grace, which is by one man, Jesus Christ, hath abounded unto many. And not as it was by one that sinned, so is the gift: for the judgment was by one to condemnation, but the free gift is of many offences unto justification. **For if by one man's offence death reigned by one; much more they which receive abundance of grace and of the gift of righteousness shall reign in life by one, Jesus Christ.** *Therefore as by the offence of one judgment came upon all men to condemnation; even so by the righteousness of one the free gift came upon all men unto justification of life. For as by one man's disobedience many were made sinners, so by the obedience of one shall many be made righteous. Moreover the law entered, that the offence might abound. But where sin abounded, grace did much more abound: that as sin hath reigned unto death, even so might grace reign through righteousness unto eternal life by Jesus Christ our Lord* (Romans 5:12-21).

After the resurrection, Jesus reiterated the same cultural mandate God gave Adam when He said:

...All power is given unto Me in heaven and in earth. Go ye therefore, and teach all nations, baptizing them in the name of the Father, and of the Son, and of the Holy Ghost: teaching them to observe all things whatsoever I have commanded you: and, lo, I

am with you always, even unto the end of the world (Matthew 28:18-20).

In Genesis 1:28, humanity is commanded to subdue the earth and have dominion. Matthew 28:18 shows how the Father gave Jesus back all the authority of Heaven as well as the earthly authority Adam failed to carry out because of disobedience. In this commission to His disciples, Jesus says this authority is for the express purpose of sending them out to teach all nations.

THE TRUTH ABOUT THE GREAT COMMISSION

There are two key words we must understand before we can make the connection between Adam and Jesus and begin to understand the truth about God's commission to humankind.

First, the word *teach* in Matthew 28:19 is the Greek word for *disciple*— μαθητεύω *matheteuo*, which means "to be a disciple of one; to follow his precepts and instructions; to make a disciple; to teach, instruct."[2]

The other word is *nations*, which in the Greek is ἔθνος *ethnos/eth·nos*, which is translated as "nation" 64 times, "heathen" five times, and "people" twice. *Vine's Bible Dictionary* defines a *nation* as a multitude (whether of men or of beasts) associated or living together; a company, troop, swarm; a multitude of individuals of the same nature or genus; the human race; a race, people group; and in the Old Testament as foreign nations not worshipping the true God, pagans or Gentiles.[3]

This verse in Matthew 28 clearly shows us that Jesus is commissioning His disciples to bring whole nations and cultures of the world under His Lordship, not just individual ethnic peoples, as most evangelicals have preached concerning our commission for over 100 years.

In other words, this means that as Christ's Church, we are not just called to minister to an individual Hispanic, Asian, Caucasian, African, or Indian person. We are called to bring the whole continents of Africa,

Antarctica, Asia, Australia, Europe, North and South America, under the influence of the Gospel. This includes their political, economic, and educational structures.

It is time we realize we are not just called to "grow churches." Christians are called collectively to manage and influence whole cities and nations by providing a biblical blueprint for every sphere of society under the rule and reign of God.

Second Corinthians 5:19 says Jesus was sent to *reconcile the world* to God: *"To wit, that God was in Christ, reconciling the world unto Himself, not imputing their trespasses unto them; and hath committed unto us the word of reconciliation."*

The Greek word for "world" is κόσμος, *kosmos* (**kos·mos**), meaning the world, the universe, and every inhabitant of the earth. It also includes the world systems, world affairs, and the whole created order, which includes far more than just individual souls.

Colossians 1:20 says Jesus came to reconcile all things back to God,

> *And, having made peace through the blood of His cross, by Him to* **reconcile all things** *unto Himself; by Him, I say, whether they be things in earth, or things in heaven.*

When God says *all*, He means **all**. *All* includes things in Heaven and on earth, natural and spiritual, not just human souls. Obviously the commission God has for humankind is much broader than we are often led to believe. We now need to learn how to accomplish this monumental assignment and train the next generation to continue on when our time is done.

THINK ON THIS

As you think on the impact each generation has on the ones to follow, consider the meanings of the following words and how they relate to your great commission as a family and as a member of the Body of Christ.

Write the definitions of these words and explain them in the context of your own life:

Generation

_____

_____

_____

Genealogy

_____

_____

_____

World

_____

_____

_____

Reconcile

_____

_____

_____

Using Genesis 1:26-28 and Matthew 28:18-20, write your own great commission as you now understand it.

_____

_____

_____

_____

_____

_____

_____

_____

ENDNOTES

1. *Strong's Exhaustive Concordance to the Bible* (Peabody, MA: Hendrickson, 2009), entry #8435.

2. *Strong's Exhaustive Concordance to the Bible* (Peabody, MA: Hendrickson, 2009), entry #3100.

3. *Thayer's Greek-English Lexicon of the New Testament* (Peabody, MA: Hendrickson, 1996), entry #1484, s.v. "ethnos."

CHAPTER 2

THE STRATEGY FOR DOMINION

And God blessed them, and God said unto them, **Be fruitful, and multiply, and replenish the earth, and subdue it***: and* **have dominion** *over the fish of the sea, and over the fowl of the air, and over every living thing that moveth upon the earth* (Genesis 1:28).

BIBLICALLY speaking, it was God's intent that all generations of the human race would be called the Generation of Blessing. When God gave humanity the cultural commission in Genesis 1:28, He blessed that first family and told them exactly how they were supposed to accomplish it. Adam and Eve chose to disobey God's direct command to them, but that does not mean His mandate was canceled.

Sociologists have coined various phrases describing contemporary generations, such as "Baby Boomers," "Baby Busters," "Generation X," and more recently some use the terms Generation Y and Z[1] because this group of young people seemed to have no purpose in life. The reason we have one generation after another known for things such as self-centeredness or lack of purpose is because they have never connected themselves to God's original intent for human existence.

It is a fact that non-religious people tend not to have as many children as religious people because many of them prefer to "enjoy" freedom rather than renounce it for the sake of children.[2]

The future belongs to the fecund and the confident. And the Islamists are both, while the West—wedded to a multiculturalism that undercuts its own confidence, a welfare state that nudges it toward sloth and self-indulgence, and a childlessness that consigns it to oblivion—is looking ever more like the ruins of a civilization.[3]

Proverbs 30:11-14 vividly describes a generation that refuses to follow God's blueprint and fulfill their great commission.

> *There is a generation that curses its father, and does not bless its mother. There is a generation that is pure in its own eyes, yet is not washed from its filthiness. There is a generation— oh, how lofty are their eyes! And their eyelids are lifted up. There is a generation whose teeth are like swords, and whose fangs are like knives, to devour the poor from off the earth, and the needy from among men (NKJV).*

Even many Christians are not experiencing the fullness of God's blessing in their lives because they are aimless and without plan or purpose. God only blesses us when we are connected to His ultimate purpose! Ephesians 1:9-11 explains how to receive the inheritance of blessings God has in place for us.

> *Having made known unto us the mystery of His will, according to His good pleasure which He hath purposed in Himself: That in the dispensation of the fullness of times He might gather together in one all things in Christ, both which are in heaven, and which are on earth; even in Him: In whom also we have obtained an inheritance, being predestinated according to the purpose of Him who worketh all things after the counsel of His own will.*

God works *all* things after the counsel of His own will, so when we work with His ultimate plan, we work with His blessing, not against it. Ephesians 1:9-11 agrees with Genesis 1:28 and Matthew 28:18-20. The cultural commission we are to pursue is the gathering of all things together in Christ, whether they are in Heaven or on the earth. So then what does the Bible teach concerning the main strategy for reaching all things for Christ?

BE FRUITFUL AND MULTIPLY

The strategy for reaching all things for Christ is found back in our key passage in Genesis 1:26-28.

> And God said, Let us make man in Our image, after Our likeness: and let them have dominion over the fish of the sea, and over the fowl of the air, and over the cattle, and over all the earth, and over every creeping thing that creepeth upon the earth. So God created man in His own image, in the image of God created He him; male and female created He them. And God blessed them, and God said unto them, **be fruitful, and multiply, and replenish the earth, and subdue it: and have dominion** over the fish of the sea, and over the fowl of the air, and over every living thing that moveth upon the earth.

Verse 28 holds some important keys to unlocking the strategy God has put in place for us to fulfill humankind's cultural commission. First of all, we are commanded to "be fruitful and multiply." In order to understand what this means, we have to remember two of the cardinal rules of biblical hermeneutics, or the science of interpreting Scripture. What was the author's original intent when he wrote it? What is the biblical context surrounding the particular verse in question?

I have heard hundreds of sermons on this verse, but I can't recall anyone presenting the main thought and original intent of the author.

WALK IN GENERATIONAL BLESSINGS

Most every preacher gives us a "spiritual" meaning of this verse, saying being fruitful and multiplying has to do with the winning of souls and the raising up of great ministries for God. Of course, you can make a case for that because you can always extract a spiritual principle from every natural command and law. First Corinthians 15:46 says, *"Howbeit that was not first which is spiritual, but that which is natural; and afterward that which is spiritual."* First comes the natural, and then the spiritual. My position is, before you can extract a spiritual meaning from a passage, you must first understand the primary literal meaning based on the context surrounding that Scripture.

Scripture must always interpret Scripture; otherwise you have no proper foundation for meaning and interpretation. Without this foundation, we are given to extreme mysticism and subjectivism which employs no standard of hermeneutics and can make a verse mean anything the reader wants it to mean! This is how many cults have started, such as Mormonism, Jehovah's Witnesses, and Islam.

For example, if the primary meaning of Genesis 1:28 is spiritual, meaning the winning of souls and having great ministries for God, then to be consistent we must say that the context of Genesis chapter 1 is also spiritual. If we apply the same definition used for verse 28, then God called the entire animal kingdom including the birds of the sky, cats, dogs, whales, insects, and even all other living things such as trees, plants, and flowers to win souls, disciple, and raise up great ministries for God! So, let me ask you:

- When was the last time you had an altar call and a water bug came up and dedicated its life to Christ?

- Have you seen a group of cows, giraffes, and whales come forward for the cause of Christ?

- Do you experience great moves of God in your ministry to the point that you see trees, birds, and plants lay on the floor for hours seeking God's face?

Before you accuse me of losing it, this is the conclusion we would have to come to if indeed we give the mandate to bear fruit and multiply. God gave humankind on the sixth day primarily a spiritual meaning. Remember, Scripture must interpret Scripture.

For us to truly understand Genesis 1:28, we have to first know what God said in Genesis 1:1-27. Clearly, the main thought presented in the preceding verses actually started on the third day of creation and remained consistent through the fifth and sixth day, the physical and biological reproduction and multiplication of each species within and according to their own kind. Referencing the plants and vegetation on the third day, we read:

> And God said, let the earth bring forth grass, the herb yielding seed, and the fruit tree yielding fruit after his kind, whose seed is in itself, upon the earth: and it was so. And the earth brought forth grass, and herb yielding seed after his kind, and the tree yielding fruit, whose seed was in itself, after his kind: and God saw that it was good. And the evening and the morning were the third day (Genesis 1:11-13).

Then, the marine life in the sea, and the fowl of the air were on the fifth day (verses 20-23):

> And God said, let the waters bring forth abundantly the moving creature that hath life, and fowl that may fly above the earth in the open firmament of heaven. And God created great whales, and every living creature that moveth, which the waters brought forth abundantly, after their kind, and every winged fowl after his kind: and God saw that it was good. And God blessed them, saying, be fruitful, and multiply, and fill the waters in the seas, and let fowl multiply in the earth. And the evening and the morning were the fifth day (Genesis 1:20-23).

The animal kingdom was created on the sixth day:

> *And God said, let the earth bring forth the living creature after his kind, cattle, and creeping thing, and beast of the earth after his kind: and it was so. And God made the beast of the earth after his kind, and cattle after their kind, and every thing that creepeth upon the earth after his kind: and God saw that it was good* (Genesis 1:24-25).

In light of this context, we can say without hesitation that God's primary call to humanity in Genesis 1:28 is to bear fruit, have biological children and multiply, have children who have children who then continue the cycle of multiplication and proliferation in the earth.

But are we just called to have many biological children?

To answer that question, we need to go back and read Genesis 1:27, *"So God created man in His own image, in the image of God created He him; male and female created He them."* Although all living things God created have the ability to bear fruit and multiply in the natural, humankind is the only one of God's creation that was created in God's own image and likeness. Therefore, we are also called to reflect God, who is Spirit (see John 4:23-24) in our natural children and the generations to come.

Before the Fall, our spirits, souls, and bodies were all aligned under God's rule! The most incredible thing we can possibly imagine in terms of God's original creation is that God put some of His DNA in each human being. I say this in human terms because nobody fully understands what this means and how God accomplished it. We are given the incredible privilege of reproducing the image of God in billions of people yet to be born in our subsequent generations! Talk about Generation Blessing—this is mind boggling!

REPLENISH THE EARTH

Genesis 1:28 also commands us not only to increase and multiply, but to replenish the earth. The Hebrew word for replenish is also translated as "fill, full, fulfill, consecrate, accomplish, overflow, and satisfy." According to *Vine's Dictionary*, replenish means "to fill, be full, fullness, abundance and to consecrate as well as to be armed, satisfied, accomplished, complete and mass up against."[4] We can use some of the primary Hebrew meanings of the word replenish to see the primary purpose of God for humankind on the earth.

Consecrate means to set something apart for God's purpose. By implication, *replenish* connotes filling the earth with God-fearing children who will set the earth apart for God.

Accomplish speaks to the fact that we are not going to accomplish the task God has given us to subdue the earth and have dominion if we neglect our biological families and neglect to prepare a legacy for the next generations.

God wants every sphere of life on planet Earth to *overflow* with His image and likeness. If we would only keep our children in the faith by teaching them biblical Christianity and affirming them in their natural and supernatural giftings, this could easily be accomplished in just two generations, even without an obvious "earth-shaking" revival.

Fulfilling this plan *satisfies* God more than the common practice of "sacrificing our families on the altar of ministry" to save folks whom we have never met before! We should endeavor to see both our families and unbelievers serve Christ! If the Church would stop aborting their children in the spirit as well as in the natural and seek to perpetuate the generational blessing God commanded in Genesis 1:28, then we would take back our nation in two to three generations!

Big events and crusades aside, we will never *complete* the mandate given to us by God without obeying the clear command in Genesis 1:28 to increase, multiply, and replenish the earth!

God is calling us to *mass up* or rise up and mount an offensive against the gates of hell primarily with the members of our families. Therefore, we can see that God's strategy to increase, multiply, and replenish the earth is through having both natural and spiritual children, who would in turn have their own children and continue this cycle until we actually populated the earth with godly seed that would incarnate the image of God. As each generation reflects His person and purpose, the whole earth would be taken for God and under His rule and Lordship.

Of course, we are all aware that since the Fall, not all in the category of "human species" have the full image and likeness of God. Thus the New Testament emphasis is to reproduce "Spiritual Children" as well as disciple our biological children. Jesus even said that in some cases the Gospel will divide physical families! (See Matthew 10:34.)

This explains how the main issue after the Fall is not just being a human being, but being "born again" and made alive spiritually. Only then can we be brought into the godly lineage of Abraham. This is also the reason why we can have "spiritual sons and daughters" who are not our natural children. People who are born again of the Spirit become Christian humans because their spirits are made alive (see 1 Cor. 15:22), their minds are renewed (see Eph. 4:23), and their bodies become the temples of the Holy Spirit (see 1 Cor. 6:15,19). They grow and begin to increase and multiply in the spiritual sense as they are *"renewed in knowledge after the image of Him that created him"* (Col. 3:10).

Since the Fall, we can also see how this principle of multiplication works in reverse to the advantage of satan's kingdom and proliferates sin and evil through the law of sowing and reaping. Galatians 6:7-8 warns us:

> *Do not be deceived, God is not mocked; for whatever a man sows, that he will also reap. For he who sows to his flesh will of the flesh reap corruption, but he who sows to the Spirit will of the Spirit reap everlasting life* (NKJV).

While the Christian Church in America sleeps and continues to lose her natural and spiritual children to the world, the kingdom of satan is gaining ground generationally. They are subsuming our culture after the devil's image and likeness and producing the "me-centered, pleasure-seeking culture" that is expounded on in Proverbs 30:11-14.

SUBDUE THE EARTH

The Hebrew meanings for *subdue* (*kabash*) is "to force, keep under or bring into bondage, dominate."[5] The Hebrew word for *dominion* is *radah*, which means "to rule, dominate, tread down, subjugate."[6] Are we subduing, ruling, and dominating the earth in the image of God? The Body of Christ is praying and fasting, doing marches, crusades, and spiritual mapping to reach our cities and nations for God. While all of these strategies are good and have had some success, the reality is that we have yet to reach one city for God! Can you believe it? As a matter of fact, even with all the various moves of God the Church has experienced since the dawn of the 20th century, we have continued to experience cultural decline at an alarming rate!

Since the early 1900s, we have seen the Welsh Revival, the Azusa Street Revival, and the birth of numerous Pentecostal denominations. We have seen the rise of healing evangelists such as Smith Wigglesworth, Charles Price, and F.F. Bosworth. Then came the Latter Rain and the Voice of Healing Movement, which reportedly saw thousands of people be healed and make decisions for Christ from 1948-1955 and featured men like T.L. Osborne, Oral Roberts, Kenneth Hagen, and Ed Coe. We saw the Charismatic Renewal Movement that swept through some of the largest Christian denominations in the world, including the Catholic church. We have witnessed the Teaching Movement in the 1970s and the mega-church movement in the 1980s. The Prophetic and Apostolic movement flourished in the 1990s, and massive moves of renewal broke out in Toronto, Pensacola, and Argentina.

The closest we have ever come to witnessing an entire American city come under the influence of the Gospel was the so-called Rochester Revival, led by Evangelist Charles Finney in 1830-1831. Since then, the Church has been losing ground to the humanistic ideologies of Darwin, Freud, Marx, and Nietzsche.

What has been our response? There is an old saying, "Expecting different results from repeatedly doing the same thing is insanity."

Crusades, events, and programs, though they are good, often take our focus off the Genesis 1:28 mandate of subduing and having dominion of the earth through the perpetuation of our generational blessing! Without the understanding of our primary focus and calling, we are unbalanced and spend more and more time within the confines of the church building. We are wearing ourselves out trying to have good meetings and events, while ignoring the larger call of managing the whole planet by raising up godly seed to be leaders in every facet of society!

OUR GREATEST HOPE

I am not against city-wide events and prayer rallies, but it is vitally important that we keep balance in our lives and keep our priorities focused on God's true mandate while we are in the midst of all our ministries. Instead of looking at our biological children as an annoyance or a hindrance to the call of God on our lives, my wife and I look at them as our primary contribution to the Great Commission and the extension of our very purpose and destiny to the next generations!

One effective strategy I have seen work well with my own children and others in our local church is to strategize with one's spouse on how to have children participate with parents in various events and ministries. Doing so will give them a burden for the Kingdom of God and provide a chance for parents to spend time with them as they are trained in serving the Lord through church and marketplace ministry! Two of my children actually gave their lives to Christ while we were conducting a street service—replete with music, drama, and preaching.

Andy Crouch gives us this powerful observation:

> If I make dinner tonight for my family, nothing much will change in my family's culture. But if I make dinner tonight, tomorrow night, next Tuesday and for the next fifteen years of our children's lives, seeking to do so with creativity, skill and grace that grows over time—even if I never become an avant-garde chef and always follow the recipe—that discipline alone will indeed create a powerful family culture with horizons of possibility and impossibility that we may not even now be able to glimpse.[7]

The greatest hope for this society in the battle against the humanistic ideologies that are permeating our culture and corrupting our children are the people who put the raising of their children as their first priority. Women in particular, who have decided *not* to listen to the feminist propaganda of self, do more to promote a productive next generation than every neuropsychologist laid end to end from here to the moon. If there is any hope for stopping the cultural decline in the United States, it is in the many intelligent, articulate women who understand that raising children is a Christian ministry.

It's starting to look like the most radical thing a Christian woman can do in the United States of America today is not to bomb an abortion clinic. The thing that will set a woman apart as a raving revolutionary is to be one who bucks the whole system of materialism and chooses to stay at home and raise her children. What she is saying to this humanistic society is, "My children are more valuable than anything the world has to offer." She is refusing to buy into the "me, myself, and I" mindset that is promoted by every facet of the media. She shows our crumbling society that her most valuable relationships are with her spouse and children because they are her true legacy.

The more I travel as a Christian activist, the more I see the number one priority for every Christian family is their own children. This is a revolution that will impact every neighborhood, city, and state in our nation for Christ!

THINK ON THIS

What five things did God command humanity to do in Genesis 1:28?

_____

_____

_____

_____

_____

How does Proverbs 30:11-14 (NKJV) describe a generation that refuses to follow God's blueprint and fulfill their great commission?

1. There is a generation that _____ its father, and does not _____ its mother.

Read Exodus 20:12. What does it say about honoring your mother and father?

_____

2. There is a generation that is pure in its _____ eyes, yet is not washed from its filthiness. There is a generation—oh, how lofty are their eyes! And their eyelids are lifted up.

This infers that pride is a problem for this generation. What does Proverbs 16:18 say about pride?

_____

_____

_____

_____

3. There is a generation whose teeth are like _____ and whose fangs are like _____, to devour the poor from off the earth, and the needy from among men.

What does Proverbs 14:31 say about those who are unkind and oppress the poor? _____

Whose image is the generation described in Proverbs 30:11-14 modeling itself after? _____

What do we need to do to make sure this is not the way of our next generations? _____

Whose image do we need to teach our children, both natural and spiritual, to model themselves after? _____

Think of ways you and your spouse can begin to include your children in your ministry.

What is God's promise to you if you obey the instructions given in Proverbs 22:6? _____

> Train up a child in the way he should go: and when he is old,
> he will not depart from it (Proverbs 22:6).

ENDNOTES

1. http://www.socialmarketing.org/newsletter/features/generation1.htm; accessed November 10, 2011.

2. From "The Rape of Europe" by Paul Belien, published online in The Brussels Journal, http://www.brusselsjournal.com/node/1609.

3. Mark Steyn, America Alone: The End of the World as We Know It (Washington: Regnery, 2001).

4. *Vine's Expository Dictionary of the Old & New Testament Words* (Nashville: Thomas Nelson, 2003).

5. *Strong's Exhaustive Concordance to the Bible* (Peabody, MA: Hendrickson, 2009).

6. Ibid.

7. Andy Crouch, *Culture Making: Recovering Our Creative Calling* (Grand Rapids, MI: InterVarsity Press, 2008), 77.

CHAPTER 3

LET'S DO THE MATH

A T the writing of this book, I have been married for more than 30 years. I and my lovely wife, Joyce, have five children from ages 13-28. I can't overstate how important the concepts in this book are to me and to my family! I owe the birth of my last two beautiful daughters to these teachings. Let me explain. Before I understood the primary focus and the divine call of God's covenant people to procreate, disciple, and train our children for cultural dominion according to Genesis 1:28, we were planning on having three children. In 1995, the lights went on, and I finally embraced this message, which motivated us to have two more children. We can't imagine our life without our two precious girls, Charissa and Rachel! They have given us some of the most joyful moments of our entire lives! Their lives and destinies are directly connected to this teaching.

When folks ask me how many children I have, they usually look shocked when I tell them. Their response is usually something like, "Wow," or "Are you serious," or "I can't believe it!" I read once that the American family at the turn of the 20th century had an average of 6.7 children per family. Now the average American family averages something in the range of 2.5 per family.[1]

CHILD-HATING HUMANISM

The reason for this marked decline is that we have bought into the self-centered lie that focuses on me, myself, and I, while completely disregarding the command and the generational blessing found in Genesis 1:28. The humanistic lie we have allowed to permeate our culture rests on the false ideologies of Darwin and Marx and the classical Greek philosophies of the Epicureans and Dionysians, which state our only purpose in this life is to live for today and be happy!

However, if we believe that there is no life after death, that there is no purpose in history, and that our only purpose in life is to fulfill our physical and bodily passions, we are no different from animals. A true disciple of Jesus, a Christian, is not called to live for the now and for immediate convenience and pleasure. We have been called to increase and multiply so we can rule and have dominion over the earth as God's ambassadors.

Consequently we live in a "child-hating culture" that sheds the innocent blood of their young by legalized murder called abortion. Even couples who don't physically abort their unborn are encouraged to plan the size of their families on the current me-centered, humanistic philosophy. They pre-plan to have a certain number of children based more on the mentality of this present "child-hating" culture than on a proper understanding of the cultural commission issued to humankind in Genesis 1:28!

It wouldn't be quite so shocking if this kind of thinking were relegated to the secular world. But I have received the same kind of shocked responses when I have revealed the size of my family to those in the Church! Even leaders and ministers give me the same response! You would think that most ministers would know at least the ABCs of the Bible, but unfortunately many don't.

I remember once speaking to an orthodox Jewish Rabbi on the phone as we worked on some pro-life issues. During the course of our conversation, he asked me how many children I had. As I told him that I had five children, I waited for the typical response I usually get from both non-Christians and Christians. When he gave no shocked response, I became curious and asked him how many children he had. His answer shocked me! He told me that he had 12 children! I responded with a "Wow." His next words shocked me even more! He told me that his family was small compared to the average Orthodox Jewish family in his area, which had 18 children! Some of his friends had 23 children! (Of course this would probably not be true for all Jewish people—especially secular Jews.)

When I asked him how he and his wife managed such a large family, he said that everything they do is centered on their generations. They put all of their children in private schools, and irrespective of whether or not they will become a rabbi, they all study at least two years in a Hebrew seminary after their graduation. They are able to finance all of this by going on inexpensive vacations and only having hand-me-down furniture.

I am not saying that every Christian should only have used furniture and aim to have 18 children, but I believe we can clearly see why the Jews have survived all the persecutions the world has brought against them. As a matter of fact, the Jewish culture has succeeded in keeping their families intact and their children in the faith! Why? Instead of seeing their children as burdens, they are the central part of each family fulfilling their destiny.

I even heard it said that in Judaism the relationship the parents have with their children is even more important than the relationship of husband and wife because their children represent their continuation to the next generation.

WHAT'S WRONG WITH THIS PICTURE?

If you look around, you can easily see how the average Christian couple has bought into this child-hating cultural lie and has effectively separated their children from their Christianity! Just look at the mess the youth are in in many of our youth ministries! Often, the children who attend Christian schools look and act no different from those who attend public schools! Why? While their parents are out five nights a week in church meetings, they leave their children at home watching television or surfing on the Internet. While we are out praying for strangers to come to Christ, our children are at home getting discipled by the MTV culture! Look at the small percentage of our young who continue to serve the Lord when they reach their teenage years. It has been my observation that the average Christian teen loses their faith by the time they graduate from college. This can't be pleasing to God! What is wrong with this picture?

Pat Buchanan wrote a book titled *The Death of the West*. One of the main themes running through his book is that while the rest of the world is continuing to have children at a rate of multiplication, the average American and Western European family averages so few children that their numbers are in decline. One reason France wasn't quick to support the United States in the war against Iraq was because the average French household is diminishing so much they actually depend on Muslim immigrants to keep the labor force at an acceptable level so the nation can continue to function![2]

If all the Christians in America would just stop aborting their children, plan to have the number of children God wants to them to have, and keep their children in the faith, just by sheer numbers we would outvote and outnumber the secular humanists in our country in just two to three generations! One of the most horrendous things I have ever read was that black babies are aborted at a rate that is three times higher than white babies![3] We are now witnessing a modern day, legalized black genocide.

Just read these statistics related to the New York City Council on November 16, 2010:

TESTIMONY OF GERARD M. NADAL, PH.D.[4]

Editorial Board, Center for Morality in Public Life

Advisory Board: Good Counsel Homes, Staten Island, New York

Honorable members of the New York City Council. As a native and lifelong resident of our city, I believe that the legislation pending before this body represents a sharp departure from this Council's honorable legacy of lifting up the socio-economically disenfranchised.

According to the New York City's 2008 Vital Statistics,[5] the following numbers of abortions have been procured between 1999-2008. In this ten-year period:

- Asian/Pacific Islander 50,382; (5.5%)

- Non-Hispanic White 101,856; (11%)

- Hispanic 296,330 (32.1%)

- Blacks (non-Hispanic) 430,515 (46.7%)

726,845 dead Black and Hispanic babies, out of the total of 922,272 in that ten-year period alone represents a *genocide in slow motion*. So do the following:

a. 20 million aborted black babies nationwide since 1973.[6]

b. The number of aborted blacks, according to the Centers for Disease Control, outnumbers the next leading seven causes of death among blacks combined.[7]

c. Blacks are down to 12.3% of the U.S. population in 2010, from 14.8% in 2000.[8]

d. While only 12.3% of the U.S. population, blacks have 37% of all abortions nationwide, and 46.7% City-wide.[9]

e. Whites in New York City have 512 abortions for every 1000 live births, Hispanics have 687 abortions per 1000 live births, and blacks have 1,260 abortions per 1000 live births. Blacks represent a race in decline.[10]

This is indeed slow motion genocide. It represents an abortion industry feeding on the poverty and fear of our neediest daughters.[11] The legislation before this body would muzzle the very resource centers who offer the hope and assistance that the abortion industry fails to furnish. This legislation is designed to preempt our offer of hope, to confirm the hopelessness of women who often lack any resource for hope in their lives; and it will railroad even greater numbers of minorities to their deaths.[12]

Am I saying that I am against birth control, contraceptives, and family planning? I leave folks to decide on their own what the Bible says about this issue. However, I will go on record as saying that I am against contraceptives that involve terminating the life of the child after conception. I will also caution men and women against doing anything permanent to their bodies that makes it impossible to have children. Many women are pressured to have their "tubes tied" during their most vulnerable time, right after they give birth. I have seen numerous women go through emotional trauma after God illuminates them with this teaching who regret permanently preventing further childbearing.

Don't allow the influence of God-hating, pleasure-seeking, nymphomaniacs like Planned Parenthood founder Margaret Sanger to determine your views on childbearing. In her work entitled *Pivot of Civilization*, Sanger espoused the thinking of eugenicists, similar to Darwin's "survival of the fittest," though she related it to the concept of human society, saying the genetic makeup of the poor and minorities, for example, was inferior. She wrote in the *Birth Control Review,* "The purpose in promoting birth control was to create a race of thoroughbreds." Sanger believed that, for the purpose of racial purification, couples should be rewarded who chose sterilization.[13]

To me, the number of children you have is between you and God. What I am saying is, don't make your decision based on a culture that views children as an inconvenience. Pray with your spouse over Genesis 1:28 in regard to your call to subdue the earth and have dominion; then make your decision with a clear conscience.

Is this the only verse on which I am basing my conclusions? No, because another important rule of biblical interpretation is that all things should be established with at least two or three witnesses and fit in with the overall major doctrines and themes of Scripture. In the next chapter we will begin a journey throughout the rest of the Bible and see how salient this theme is throughout.

But before we move on, let us look at a powerful article entitled "The Liberal Baby Bust," by Phillip Longman.[14]

In this article, Longman predicts a conservative fundamentalist future based on the comparable birth demographics between liberals and conservatives. For example, Longman states:

> Today, fertility correlates strongly with a wide range of political, cultural, and religious attitudes. In the USA, for example, 47% of people who attend church weekly say their ideal family size is three or more children. By contrast, 27% of those who seldom attend church want that many kids.
>
> In Utah, where more than two-thirds of residents are members of The Church of Jesus Christ of Latter-day Saints, 92 children are born each year for every 1,000 women,

the highest fertility rate in the nation. By contrast Vermont—the first to embrace gay unions—has the nation's lowest rate, producing 51 children per 1,000 women....

Similarly, in Europe today, the people least likely to have children are those most likely to hold progressive views of the world...Do you find soft drugs, homosexuality, and euthanasia acceptable? Do you seldom, if ever, attend church? Europeans who answer affirmatively to such questions are far more likely to live alone or be in childless, cohabiting unions than are those who answer negatively.

This correlation between secularism, individualism, and low fertility portends a vast change in modern societies.

Longman also notes that single-child families are on their way to extinction because a single-child only replaces one, not both of the parents. A growing segment of our modern secular society is having families smaller than needed for the birth rate to exceed the death rate.

Longman's conclusion is that American culture will drift toward social conservatism only because conservatives will outnumber their progressive secular counterparts.

THINK ON THIS

The best way to discover God's heart on any issue is to search His Word, the Bible.

Below is a list of Scriptures concerning children and family. As you read each one, put it in your own words and record whatever revelation you receive concerning what God says about children and family.

Deuteronomy 4:9

Psalm 78:4-6

Psalm 103:13-18

Psalm 127:3

Proverbs 17:6

Proverbs 29:15

Jeremiah 32:38-39

Mark 10:14

Ephesians 6:1-4

It's impossible to parent part-time. Parenting requires our full-time attention, love, care, discipline, effort, and excellence. Too often we try to squeeze parenting into a rushed, stressed schedule of work, recreation, personal development, entertainment, and overlapping activities. Parenting rooted in God's truth is a precious legacy. Parenting creates a sweet taste and a hunger for God.[15]

ENDNOTES

1. Pat Buchanan, *The Death of the West* (New York: Thomas Dunne Books, 2001).

2. Ibid.

3. Center for Disease Control, Surveillance Summaries, November 28, 2003/52 (SS12), 1-32; located online at http://www.cdc.gov/mmwr/preview/mmwrhtml/ss5212a1.htm.

4. Gerard M. Nadal, http://www.gerardnadal.com/2010/11/16/testifying-the-power-of-the-holy-spirit-part-i/.

5. Summary of Vital Statistics 2008, City of New York, http://www.nyc.gov/html/doh/downloads/pdf/vs/2008sum.pdf; accessed July 7, 2011.

6. L. Tolbert, "Over 20 Million Aborted: Why Planned Parenthood Targets the Inner-City"; http://www.civilrightsfoundation.

org/pdfs/tolbert_plannedparenthood_targets.pdf; accessed July 7, 2011).

7. Gamble, et al. "Abortion Surveillance, United States, 2005," *Morbidity and Mortality Weekly Reports*, Nov. 28, 2008/57 (SS 13); 1-32; http://www.cdc.gov/mmwr/preview/mmwrhtml/ ss5713a1.htm?s_cid=ss5713a1_e#tab9; accessed July 7, 2011.

8. "The Black Population in the United States," *U.S. Census Bureau*; http://www.census.gov/population/www/socdemo/race/ black.html; accessed July 7, 2011.

9. "Summary of Vital Statistics 2008, City of New York"; http:// www.nyc.gov/html/doh/downloads/pdf/vs/2008sum.pdf; accessed July 7, 2011; Gamble, et al. "Abortion Surveillance, United States, 2005," *Morbidity and Mortality Weekly Reports*, Nov. 28, 2008/57 (SS 13); 1-32; http://www.cdc.gov/mmwr/ preview/mmwrhtml/ss5713a1.htm?s_cid=ss5713a1_e#tab9; accessed July 7, 2011.

10. "Table 23: Induced Abortion and Abortion Ratios by Race, Ethnicity and Resident County New York State – 2008"; http:// www.health.state.ny.us/nysdoh/vital_statistics/2008/table23. htm; accessed July 7, 2011.

11. L. Tolbert, "Over 20 Million Aborted: Why Planned Parenthood Targets the Inner-City"; http://www.civilrightsfoundation. org/pdfs/tolbert_plannedparenthood_targets.pdf; accessed July 7, 2011.

12. "Maafa 21: Black Genocide in 21st Century America," produced by Life Dynamics, released 2009. This is a detailed documentary film on the history of the eugenics movement in America, its effects on the African American community, and the role played by Margaret Sanger and Planned Parenthood.

13. David Kennedy, *Birth Control in America, The Career of Margaret Sanger* (New Haven, CT: Yale University Press, 1970), 117, quoting a 1923 Sanger speech.

14. Phillip Longman, "The Liberal Baby Bust," published in *USA Today*, March 13, 2006.

15. Dr. Larry Keefauver, *77 Irrefutable Truths of Parenting* (Alachua, FL: Bridge-Logos, 2003).

CHAPTER 4

TRACING THE GODLY SEED

And I will put enmity between thee and the woman, and between thy seed and her Seed; it shall bruise thy head, and thou shalt bruise His heel (Genesis 3:15).

GOD'S plan of redemption through families didn't end with the Fall of humanity in the Garden. Instead of scrapping the plan altogether, God continued planning for generational dominion, except now it would have to culminate in Messiah, the last Adam.

Although God could have sent His Son immediately to crush satan, He still chose to wage war and accomplish His will by generations of obedient disciples.

THE STORY OF NOAH

But Noah found grace in the eyes of the Lord. These are the generations of Noah: Noah was a just man and perfect in his generations, and Noah walked with God. And Noah begat three sons, Shem, Ham, and Japheth (Genesis 6:8-10).

When Noah found grace in the eyes of the Lord, the Bible describes him as *"a just man and **perfect in his generations**."* The Bible never separated this man God used to spare humanity from his generations. When Noah was mentioned, his children were mentioned in the same context. When God spoke to Noah about covenant and about the ark, He included Noah's family in that covenant and plan of salvation.

> But with thee will I establish My covenant; and thou shalt come into the ark, thou, and thy sons, and thy wife, and thy sons' wives with thee (Genesis 6:18).

I wonder what Noah would think about the followers of God today who very rarely see the connection between themselves and their generations!

The first covenant God made with Noah after the flood was a reiteration of the original covenant of creation He made with Adam in Genesis 1:28.

> And **God blessed Noah and his sons**, and said unto them, **be fruitful, and multiply, and replenish the earth.** And the fear of you and the dread of you shall be upon every beast of the earth, and upon every fowl of the air, upon all that moveth upon the earth, and upon all the fishes of the sea; into your hand are they delivered (Genesis 9:1-2).

The only real difference between this covenant and the original covenant with Adam in Genesis 1:28 is that God was able to get more specific and include Noah's sons in the Noahic Covenant. This is very important for all to grasp so we do not believe those who say the original covenant of dominion God made with Adam was done away with after the Fall!

THE GENERATIONAL CURSE

To conclude this story on Noah, let's look at Genesis 9:20-27.

> And Noah began to be an husbandman, and he planted a vineyard: And he drank of the wine, and was drunken; and he was

uncovered within his tent. And Ham, the father of Canaan, saw the nakedness of his father, and told his two brethren without. And Shem and Japheth took a garment, and laid it upon both their shoulders, and went backward, and covered the nakedness of their father; and their faces were backward, and they saw not their father's nakedness.

And Noah awoke from his wine, and knew what his younger son had done unto him. And he said, Cursed be Canaan; a servant of servants shall he be unto his brethren. And he said, Blessed be the Lord God of Shem; and Canaan shall be his servant. God shall enlarge Japheth, and he shall dwell in the tents of Shem; and Canaan shall be his servant.

This passage recalls the time when Noah got drunk, disrobed, and lay on his bed. His son Ham uncovered his father's nakedness by reporting it to his two brothers, Shem and Japheth. Shem and Japheth responded by walking backward and covering Noah. What were the consequences for Ham's act of dishonoring his father? Well, if you think like the typical person who only lives for the moment, you wouldn't think it was such a big deal. Nothing happened immediately to Ham. As far as we know, he lived in peace and prosperity in his lifetime. But when you think in terms of the biblical understanding of generations, the consequences Ham suffered were horrific! The descendants of Ham's son, Canaan, became slaves or servants of the descendants of Shem and Japheth when the nation of Israel conquered the land of Canaan!

The generational principle shown here is that when you dishonor your past by dishonoring your parents, you curse your future! The fifth of the Ten Commandments reads, *"Honour thy father and thy mother: that thy days may be long upon the land which the Lord thy God giveth thee"* (Exod. 20:12). Whether we like it or not, we are all part of an intergenerational connection, whether it is for good (generational blessing) or for evil (generational curse).

THE STORY OF ABRAHAM

> *Now the Lord had said unto Abram, Get thee out of thy country, and from thy kindred, and from thy father's house, unto a land that I will shew thee: And I will make of thee a great nation, and I will bless thee, and make thy name great; and thou shalt be a blessing: And I will bless them that bless thee, and curse him that curseth thee: and **in thee shall all families of the earth be blessed*** (Genesis 12:1-3).

In the story of Abraham we again see the Lord referring back to the original cultural mandate found in the covenant of creation in Genesis 1:28. The first time God gave this mandate to Adam, it was very general. The next time God gave it to Noah, it was still very general because God had to start everything again from scratch because of the flood.

In the story of Abraham, God was able to get more specific by keeping a godly seed long enough to build upon the original covenant. Though the language is a bit different, we still see the same main elements of affecting the nations with the blessing and rule of God through His people. Everything God told Abraham had to do with generations! First, in verse 1, Abram had to break a generational curse by leaving his idolatrous past: his father's house, his country, and his people. Once Abram obeyed this command, God could give him a glorious future and make of him a great nation. God is dealing with the generations, Abram's past and his future.

God then shows Abram specifically how He is going to do this through Abram and his future generations. *"In you **all** the **families** of the earth shall be blessed!"* God was going to use Abram to begin a generational blessing that would positively affect every family on the earth. When God says all, He means all! Because of God's emphasis on the generations, He had to use families to carry the blessing of the Gospel to the ends of the earth!

When reading the story of Abraham, we can easily observe that it's a narrative of his family's story. There were some good accounts and some bad accounts; but the most important thing to understand is that God worked through Abram's family to bring about the fulfillment of blessing the earth with the coming of Messiah!

Genesis 12:7 reads:

> *The Lord appeared unto Abram, and said, Unto thy seed [children/descendents] will I give this land: and there builded he an altar unto the Lord, who appeared unto him.*

Then in Genesis 13:15-17 it says:

> *For all the land which thou seest, to thee will I give it, **and to thy seed forever**. And I will make thy seed as the dust of the earth: so that if a man can number the dust of the earth, then shall thy seed also be numbered. Arise, walk through the land in the length of it and in the breadth of it; for I will give it unto thee.*

It is important to note that when God told Abram that He would give him the land of Canaan, He was referring to Abram's seed! This makes no sense to those who are locked into a time and space mentality based on the "give me mine now" culture! Abram never owned or conquered the whole land of Canaan, yet God promised him the land! This is difficult to comprehend if we look at it only from the current evangelical mindset that insists that we have to experience revival in every facet of society in our lifetime or we've failed! The truth is that the biblical blueprint for success is always intergenerational.

When we first read Genesis 15:13-16, we tend to look at it as a negative in Abraham's future.

> *And he said unto Abram, Know of a surety that thy seed shall be a stranger in a land that is not theirs, and shall serve them; and they shall afflict them four hundred years; and also that nation, whom they shall serve, will I judge: and afterward shall they come out with great substance. And thou salt go to thy*

fathers in peace; thou salt be buried in a good old age. But in the fourth generation they shall come hither again: for the iniquity of the Amorites is not yet full.

Can you imagine God's plan for your success not allowing you to see its fullness and victory? What if God told you that His plan for success included 400 years of slavery?

To Abram it was filled with redemptive power because God predicted that his seed would come out of bondage and experience the Promised Land in the fourth generation! *Lord, please give us, Your people, the generational understanding needed to plan for real success!*

Genesis 17:5-9 explains the concept of multiple generational blessing even in the changing of Abram's name to Abraham.

*Neither shall thy name any more be called Abram, but thy name shall be Abraham; for a father of many nations have I made thee. And I will make thee exceeding fruitful, and I will make nations of thee, and kings shall come out of thee. And I will establish My covenant between Me and thee and thy **seed** after thee in their **generations** for an everlasting covenant, to be a God unto thee, and to thy **seed** after thee. And I will give unto thee and to thy **seed** after thee, the land wherein thou art a stranger, all the land of Canaan, for an everlasting possession; and I will be their God. And God said unto Abraham, Thou shalt keep My covenant therefore, thou, and thy **seed** after thee in their **generations**.*

Note how many times God uses the words *seed* and *generations* in His dealing with Abraham. The covenant of creation for dominion here continues to get more specific as God not only promises Abraham that nations will come out of him, but also Kings or Rulers! His "seed" is not to be content just to coexist on this planet; they are called to manage and lead the planet! Who do you think Abraham's "seed" is in today's world? Are we managing and leading this planet for God as we have been instructed to?

THE COVENANT OF CIRCUMCISION: THE SIGN UPON OUR GENERATIONS

The Old Testament sign of the covenant between God and the people of Israel was circumcision. This was God's way of marking His people for generations. A male child born in a Jewish house was required to receive this mark when he was only 8 days old, and it was the direct responsibility of the father. To see how God makes a connection between the generations, a person who was not circumcised would be cut off from among the people. Here, God judges the son for a sin of the father!

> *And God said unto Abraham, Thou shalt keep My covenant therefore, thou, and thy **seed** after thee in their **generations**. This is My covenant, which ye shall keep, **between Me and you and thy seed after thee**; every man child among you shall be circumcised. And ye shall circumcise the flesh of your foreskin; and it shall be a token of the covenant betwixt Me and you. And he that is eight days old shall be circumcised among you, every man child in your generations, he that is born in the house, or bought with money of any stranger, which is not of thy seed. He that is born in thy house, and he that is bought with thy money, must needs be circumcised: and My covenant shall be in your flesh for an everlasting covenant. And the uncircumcised man child whose flesh of his foreskin is not circumcised, that soul shall be cut off from his people; he hath broken My covenant (Genesis 17:9-14).*

The New Testament equivalent of circumcision is the rite of water baptism. Baptism officially brings a person into the covenant with God through Jesus Christ. There is controversy on whether infants should be baptized because of the Old Testament rite of circumcision. The question disputed here is whether or not an infant can come into covenant with God before the age of accountability. Whatever your point of view, we have to understand that in both covenants God requires a seal or sign of a generational covenant between Him and His people. Our children should be officially brought into covenant with God as soon as possible, whether it is done through the rite of water baptism or the rite of baby dedication.

Why did God choose Abraham to be the father of all who believe? Most of us would probably answer by saying it was because he had so much faith, courage, and passion. The answer is found in Genesis 18:18-19.

> *Seeing that Abraham shall surely become a great and mighty nation, and all the nations of the earth shall be blessed in him?* **For I know him, that he will command his children and his household after him, and they shall keep the way of the Lord, to do justice and judgment;** *that the Lord may bring upon Abraham that which He hath spoken of him.*

God chose Abraham because He knew it wouldn't be a waste of time! He knew that Abraham would pass on to his generations the things that God spoke to him. I wonder how many folks God has passed by and not given great tasks because they only thought in terms of one generation.

THE STORY OF SODOM AND GOMORRAH

As we continue our study in Genesis, we find the story of Sodom and Gomorrah, which illustrates the antithesis of generational thinking. Why did God destroy Sodom and Gomorrah? From reading all the accounts that describe these two cities, it's obvious that homosexuality was rampant; it was a blatantly homosexual culture!

> *But before they lay down, the* **men of the city, even the men of Sodom, compassed the house round, both old and**

> **young, all the people from every quarter**: And they called
> unto Lot, and said unto him, Where are the men which came
> in to thee this night? **Bring them out unto us, that we may
> know them** (Genesis 19:4-5).

What is the main challenge related to homosexuality? Any culture that allows homosexuality or even heterosexual promiscuity to dominate its culture ensures that it has no future! God cut them off because they had already cut themselves off from their destiny and their future.

God curses one-generational thinking. He will never allow that kind of mindset to prevail in the earth.[1] Why? Homosexuality embodies the quintessential of the "I, Me, My" way of life in terms of not living or planning for future generations. The human race would have been extinct a long time ago if every human practiced homosexuality! Same-sex couples cannot produce their own children, so even with artificial insemination, it is impossible for said couples to give birth to their very own biological children. Only one parent at a time can experience it, thus ensuring the generational death of their union.

Conversely, if everybody in any given society actually practiced the moral code of the Bible, using the Ten Commandments as the standard for their culture, that society would continue in peace and harmony and experience blessings for generations.

The average homosexual doesn't live as long as that person's contemporaries. This is because most homosexuals have multiple partners and regularly engage in the most unhealthy, unsafe sex act in terms of contracting sexually transmitted diseases, including HIV. Consequently, the average homosexual male in America only lives to be in his 40s.[2] This is a tragedy my family has experienced firsthand. Two of my first cousins were practicing homosexuals and died of AIDS in their mid-40s.

A young man whom I led to the Lord and who attended our local church for more than ten years died at the age of 32 from the AIDS virus contracted through continual homosexual encounters. He told me that it was a lifestyle so addictive that he would often go into public bathrooms in the subways to have sex with strangers. Several weeks before he contracted the virus, he was backslidden and living in sin. I had been praying for him and warned him prophetically that if he had one more homosexual encounter he was going to sin the sin of death as spoken of in First John 5:16. I told him I didn't know if that meant he would lose his salvation or he would contract a deadly disease.

He hung up on me and didn't listen to me. We didn't speak again until a few weeks later when he called me and said that he had continued having sex with strangers, even after I warned him, and had just found out he had the AIDS virus. Since that was in the late 1980s, they didn't have the medication available today to prolong the life of those with AIDS. Within a year and a half, this young man died a horrible and very painful death! Thank God, after he contracted the disease he repented and served the Lord. I watched helplessly as he withered away, but I am thankful to God that I will meet him again one day in His blessed Kingdom.

Did you ever wonder why the homosexual lobby is pro-choice in regard to abortion? If they don't have biological children, why do they even care about abortion? I believe they are of the mindset that if child-killing and infanticide through abortion are legally allowed, society will eventually allow any other previously illegal practice. After all, if society allows legal bloodletting of millions of innocent lives because of the so-called "right" of the mother, then there will be no limits as to the rights it will grant its citizens.

The militant homosexual lobby[3] currently influencing our media, the courts, and our elected officials are not just looking for equality. I believe they desire to dominate every aspect of life until our nation becomes a homosexual nation. Make no mistake about it; the nature of the gay lifestyle demands that the ideas of homosexuality be pushed in the media, in the public school system, and in every arena available. It is a fight for their survival! Because they cannot perpetuate themselves biologically, it must be done through the realm of ideas and worldviews.

A cultural war is presently being waged that is more important than the war on terrorism or any other war we can imagine! It is a war for the soul of America! For their ideas to survive, *militant* homosexuals must push for moral relativism, diversity, and redefining our nation's concept of *liberty* to mean freedom from all moral restraints. Their ideas are opposed to that of Bible-believing Christians and all religious and non-religious persons who believe in moral absolutes.

If you want to see what happens when a majority of people espouse homosexuality as their praxis and practice in a city, read the story of Sodom and Gomorrah in Genesis 19:13,24-25:

> *For we will destroy this place, because the cry of them is waxen great before the face of the Lord; and the Lord hath sent us to destroy it. Then the Lord rained upon Sodom and upon Gomorrah brimstone and fire from the Lord out of heaven; And He overthrew those cities, and all the plain, and all the inhabitants of the cities, and that which grew upon the ground.*

In spite of the destruction of Sodom and Gomorrah, the seed of God continued on through Abraham and his offspring. The redemption of God and subsequent victory for God's covenant people was again stated just a few chapters later in Genesis 22:15-18:

> *And the angel of the Lord called unto Abraham out of heaven the second time, And said, By Myself have I sworn, saith the Lord, for because thou hast done this thing, and hast not withheld thy son, thine only son: That in blessing I will bless thee, and in multiplying I will multiply thy **seed** as the stars of the heaven, and as the sand which is upon the sea shore; and **thy seed shall possess the gate of his enemies**; And in **thy seed** shall all the nations of the earth be blessed; because thou hast obeyed My voice.*

The plan of God to affect culture through the proliferation of godly seed, which was first given to Adam in Genesis 1:28, now culminates in a very specific prophetic word from the Lord. The seed of Abraham will actually rule the gates of its enemies. God has a multi-generational plan that includes His people influencing the political, social, and economic realms in all the heathen nations.

The promise is repeated again in Genesis 24:60 to Rebekah, the future wife of Abraham's son Isaac. *"And they blessed Rebekah, and said unto her, Thou art our sister, be thou the mother of thousands of millions, and **let thy seed possess the gate of those which hate them**."* Notice how the same prophetic words were handed down generationally!

Nowadays, we get discouraged if prophetic words aren't fulfilled in a few years. The prophetic words we receive should be kept in a journal and handed down to our natural and spiritual children. Many of these prophecies are for the generations yet to come!

PROPHETIC WORDS GIVEN TO THE GENERATIONS

As we continue our study of the generations through Genesis, it is important to understand the relevance of journaling and passing down prophecy to the next generation.

Isaac gave these prophetic words to Jacob in Genesis 27:29:

> *Let people serve thee, and nations bow down to thee: be lord over thy brethren, and let thy mother's sons bow down to thee: cursed be every one that curseth thee, and blessed be he that blesseth thee.*

In Genesis 28:3-4 Isaac again called for Jacob to give him a generational blessing:

> *And God Almighty bless thee, and make thee fruitful, and multiply thee, that thou mayest be a multitude of people; And*

give thee the blessing of Abraham, to thee, and to thy seed with thee; that thou mayest inherit the land wherein thou art a stranger, which God gave unto Abraham.

In Genesis 28:13-14, Jacob was given the same generational blessing by God Himself:

And, behold, the Lord stood above it, and said, I am the Lord God of Abraham thy father, and the God of Isaac: the land whereon thou liest, to thee will I give it, and to thy seed; And thy seed shall be as the dust of the earth, and thou shalt spread abroad to the west, and to the east, and to the north, and to the south: and in thee and in thy seed shall all the families of the earth be blessed.

Another prophecy is given to Jacob by God in Genesis 35:10-12:

And God said unto him, Thy name is Jacob: thy name shall not be called any more Jacob, but Israel shall be thy name: and he called his name Israel. And God said unto him, I am God Almighty: be fruitful and multiply; a nation and a company of nations shall be of thee, and kings shall come out of thy loins; And the land which I gave Abraham and Isaac, to thee I will give it, and to thy seed after thee will I give the land.

The generational blessing perpetuated by the godly seed first mentioned in Genesis 3:15 was so important to Jacob that he adopted Joseph's two sons so that they could both continue the godly line. We see this first in Genesis 48:3-5:

And Jacob said unto Joseph, God Almighty appeared unto me at Luz in the land of Canaan, and blessed me, and said unto me, Behold, I will make thee fruitful, and multiply thee, and I will make of thee a multitude of people; and will give this land to thy seed after thee for an everlasting possession. And now

thy two sons, Ephraim and Manasseh, which were born unto
thee in the land of Egypt before I came unto thee into Egypt,
are mine; as Reuben and Simeon, they shall be mine.

Joseph was so mindful of perpetuating the generational blessing that he allowed two of his sons to be transferred over to his father Jacob so that they could be in the direct line of the blessing of Abraham, Isaac, and Jacob. In this way, Joseph was really receiving a double portion because his success was identified with his seed! In Genesis 48:14-16, Joseph's two sons received the generational blessing directly from Jacob, now called Israel:

And Israel stretched out his right hand, and laid it upon
Ephraim's head, who was the younger, and his left hand upon
Manasseh's head, guiding his hands wittingly; for Manasseh
was the firstborn. And he blessed Joseph, and said, God, before
whom my fathers Abraham and Isaac did walk, the God which
fed me all my life long unto this day, the Angel which redeemed
me from all evil, bless the lads; and let my name be named on
them, and the name of my fathers Abraham and Isaac; and let
them grow into a multitude in the midst of the earth.

Unlike the "I, Me, My Generation" of today, Joseph didn't care much about his own personal suffering. He was more interested in preserving the blessing of God upon his family and their godly seed. Read the following passage in Genesis 50:17-21 that shows the profound way Joseph answered his brothers when they came to him because they feared for their lives:

So shall ye say unto Joseph, Forgive, I pray thee now, the tres-
pass of thy brethren, and their sin; for they did unto thee evil:
and now, we pray thee, forgive the trespass of the servants of
the God of thy father. And Joseph wept when they spake unto
him. And his brethren also went and fell down before his face;

and they said, Behold, we be thy servants. And Joseph said unto them, Fear not: for am I in the place of God? But as for you, ye thought evil against me; but God meant it unto good, to bring to pass, as it is this day, to save much people alive. Now therefore fear ye not: I will nourish you, and your little ones. And he comforted them, and spake kindly unto them.

In Genesis 50:22-25 we see that Joseph lived life as a continuum of the generational blessing and plan of God:

...Joseph lived an hundred and ten years. And Joseph saw Ephraim's children of the third generation: the children also of Machir the son of Manasseh were brought up upon Joseph's knees. And Joseph said unto his brethren, I die: and God will surely visit you, and bring you out of this land unto the land which he sware to Abraham, to Isaac, and to Jacob. And Joseph took an oath of the children of Israel, saying, God will surely visit you, and ye shall carry up my bones from hence.

Perhaps we can now understand how Joseph was able to keep himself pure and walk with integrity before God in spite of all the adverse circumstances he experienced throughout his early life. (See Genesis 37–45.) He always connected his past, present, and future, giving him a glorious vision of God's plan for his generations! Those who selfishly choose to live for the moment will cower in a corner and give up the instant the trials of life hit! Those who don't have an understanding of the generational blessing will not understand the generational consequences for their selfish, negative actions.

We will only be able to persevere through the tests and trials of today because we are anchored in the accomplishments of God in the past that sustain and propel us into our glorious future!

THINK ON THIS

Review this chapter and give the biblical definition of:

Generational Blessing:

_____

_____

Generational Curse:

_____

_____

As you read about the various families spoken of in Genesis, explain how what you learned relates to you and your family's generational blessings and/or curses.

Noah

Abram/Abraham

Jacob/Israel

Joseph

Are there generational "curses" you need to put an end to so that they are not passed on to the next generation? Explain:

_____

_____

_____

_____

What are the generational blessings you want to pass on to your next generation?

_____

_____

How are you going to accomplish this?

_____

_____

Read Jeremiah 32:38-41. What are God's promises to you as a family in these verses?

_____

_____

_____

_____

What do you have to do to attain these generational blessings?

_____

_____

_____

_____

ENDNOTES

1. I have been in close relationship with many who identified themselves as gay; thus I am not against these individuals per

se, but against the militant homosexual agenda that is trying to transmute our nation into a gay nation in the same way I am against the purveyors of heterosexual promiscuity in pop culture who regularly attempt to sexualize our children through music and all forms of media. Hence, I am against any attempt to sexualize our nation outside of the sacred biblical union between one man and one woman in traditional marriage.

2. Michael M. Bates, "Homosexual life expectancy and the gay agenda," Wednesday, June 8, 2005. A press release from the Family Research Institute announces a study that purportedly "provides additional evidence that the practice of homosexuality, with its attendant lifestyle, shortens the life of practitioners by about 20 years." This is the sort of news that will absolutely, positively make some people less than gay. Titled "Gay obituaries closely track officially reported deaths from AIDS," study results will appear in the journal *Psychological Reports*. The president of the Family Research Institute, Paul Cameron, led the project. The latest report builds on an earlier one in which Dr. Cameron examined deaths reported in homosexual publications, tracked the ages of the deceased, and averaged the results. The life expectancy of a male homosexual, it was determined, was in the early 40s.

3. The militant gay agenda probably only makes up 2-3 percent of those who identify themselves as gay; the majority of those who practice homosexuality don't attempt to impose their lifestyle on the population, and many of them probably cringe at some of the same things we are alarmed with regarding the militant gay agenda. (I liken it to the way we in the evangelical church cringe when members of the Westboro Baptist Church have the audacity to protest at the funerals of young servicemen slain while serving our nation. I also think of that loose cannon pastor from Florida, Terry Jones, who gained infamy when he threatened to burn copies of the Koran. These people don't speak for me, and they don't speak for the overwhelming majority of Christians!)

CHAPTER 5

KEEPING FAITH IN THE JOURNEY

And all the souls that came out of the loins of Jacob were seventy souls: for Joseph was in Egypt already. And Joseph died, and all his brethren, and all that generation. And the children of Israel were fruitful, and increased abundantly, and multiplied, and waxed exceeding mighty; and the land was filled with them. Now there arose up a new king over Egypt, which knew not Joseph. And he said unto his people, Behold, the people of the children of Israel are more and mightier than we: Come on, let us deal wisely with them; lest they multiply, and it come to pass, that, when there falleth out any war, they join also unto our enemies, and fight against us, and so get them up out of the land. Therefore they did set over them taskmasters to afflict them with their burdens. And they built for Pharaoh treasure cities, Pithom and Raamses. But the more they afflicted them, the more they multiplied and grew. And they were grieved because of the children of Israel (Exodus 1:5-12).

THOSE who follow the dictates of the original cultural mandate in Genesis 1:28 will experience the maximum blessing of God irrespective of their circumstances. People who allow economic reasons to stop them from believing God will provide for the amount of children He wants them to have are missing the miraculous provision that awaits all who obey. Remember, God *"blessed them and said unto them, be fruitful* [have children] *and multiply* [generations of children]*."*

As Abraham found out, you can't curse what God has blessed! In the beginning of the Exodus story, we see how the children of Israel obeyed even though they were in a foreign land. It tells us in 1:7, *"the children of Israel were **fruitful, and increased abundantly, and multiplied,** and waxed exceeding mighty; and **the land was filled with them**,"* which sounds just like the Genesis 1:28 mandate. One man, Jacob, became 70 people, then infiltrated and filled an entire nation!

If the evangelical church in America stopped aborting their destiny by killing or stopping the birth of their God-ordained children, then discipled and kept them in the faith, we could fill America with godly leadership and have the largest voting block in the nation within two generations. That is the surefire way to take back our nation!

When did the trouble start for the children of Israel? Exodus 1:8 says, *"Now there arose up a new king over Egypt, which knew not Joseph."* The Egyptians turned against the children of Israel because they forsook the generational connection they had with Joseph! They forgot that it was this man and his God who spared them during the famine and allowed them to continue as a nation!

We have a similar situation in the United States today with the liberal elite and intellectuals rewriting the history books so that all mention of Christianity would be effaced from our memory. Just like the Egyptians who forgot the God and the people who saved their land, the current crop of leadership in secular media and in higher education have turned their backs on and are attempting to destroy both the God and the people of God who made this nation great. I heard one man say, "It's like the child slapping the face of his father while sitting on his lap. Of course, the only way the child can be within reach of his father's face is to be propped up on his lap!"

Exodus 1:12 explains the result of the Egyptian persecution on Israel; *"But the more they afflicted them, the more they multiplied and grew...."* When we obey the purpose statement given to us in Genesis 1:28, we will prosper and be blessed in spite of all adversity! It doesn't matter whether we live in the city or in a rough environment or in challenging economic times; God has already promised to bless us if we stand firm in covenant with Him!

Affliction and persecution can never stop faithful believers from advancing. The first three centuries of its existence, the Church was persecuted under the Roman emperors, yet it continued to grow until the Edict of Milan in A.D. 313, which granted Christianity the right to exist and paved the way for the whole empire to be Christianized.

A more recent illustration is in Communist China when, in 1949, they expunged the country of all foreign missionaries. Then throughout the period called the Cultural Revolution, the government attempted to wipe Christianity totally out of their country. They destroyed Bibles and churches and martyred or imprisoned thousands of Christians. When the persecution started in the early 1950s, there were only about one million Christians in China. In spite of this dire persecution, one generation later they had between 70-100 million believers. Some estimates go as high as saying there are 200 million Christians living in China. Many are saying that China will be fully Christianized by the year 2050!

Perhaps the Body of Christ in the United States needs a healthy dose of persecution to wake us up and renew our passion for Christ! God may be allowing an erosion of freedom because we seem to be not taking advantage of our religious liberty. Instead of being focused on the mission of the Church to disciple all nations, we are inwardly focused and only concerned about maintaining our life comforts. Soon it may be illegal to preach from all the words of the Bible because of hate speech legislation. In the next decade, churches may be required to marry same-sex couples or face stiff penalties. If we are not careful and wake up to what is really going on in our country, we may fall prey to the primary plan of satan!

THE PRIMARY PLAN OF SATAN

And the king of Egypt spake to the Hebrew midwives, of which the name of the one was Shiphrah, and the name of the other Puah: And he said, When ye do the office of a midwife to the Hebrew women, and see them upon the stools; if it be a son, then ye shall kill him: but if it be a daughter, then she shall live. But the midwives feared God, and did not as the king of Egypt commanded them, but saved the men children alive. And the king of Egypt called for the midwives, and said unto them, Why have ye done this thing, and have saved the men children alive? And the midwives said unto Pharaoh, Because the Hebrew women are not as the Egyptian women; for they are lively, and are delivered ere the midwives come in unto them. Therefore God dealt well with the midwives: and the people multiplied, and waxed very mighty. And it came to pass, because the midwives feared God, that he made them houses. And Pharaoh charged all his people, saying, Every son that is born ye shall cast into the river, and every daughter ye shall save alive (Exodus 1:15-22).

I believe that the primary strategy satan has employed to stop us from evangelizing the world is to destroy the generational blessing of the Church. This can be seen corporately in the past corruption of the Roman Catholic church, which resulted in the fragmentation of the Church manifest in the Protestant Reformation and its numerous denominations. This can be seen in families as well when we see the children of Christians captivated by the god of this world and flowing with all its related systems and fashions.

Pharaoh was smart. He knew that the only way to defeat the children of Israel was to have a *generational plan of conquest*. He let them keep their religion and their lives. He only wanted their firstborn sons! Why the focus on the firstborn son? In the Jewish culture, the firstborn received a double portion of the inheritance of the family and became the head of the family when the father died. The bloodline of the family is passed on through the father into his sons. Killing the firstborn son destroys the one with the double portion of God's blessing and inheritance and takes out the one called to lead and manage the next generation of leaders and family members. The bloodline that carries and creates life for the generations to come is effectively cut off.

Satan attempted this same strategy later on in Exodus 10:8-11 when Pharaoh was negotiating with Moses and told him that he and the men could go and worship their God, but they had to leave their wives and children behind!

> *And Moses and Aaron were brought again unto Pharaoh: and he said unto them, Go, serve the Lord your God: but who are they that shall go? And Moses said, We will go with our young and with our old, with our sons and with our daughters, with our flocks and with our herds will we go; for we must hold a feast unto the Lord. And he said unto them, Let the Lord be so with you, as I will let you go, and your little ones: look to it; for evil is before you. Not so: go now ye that are men, and serve the Lord; for that ye did desire....*

To the Jews, worship involved the whole family. How sad it is that many in the Church today have fallen for this very trap of satan! Pharaoh was willing to let the men go to worship, but Moses would not have it. In the overall picture of a local church, the family has to be the center of the focus in terms of ministry. Any church that has a continual schedule that demands their congregation attend five nights a week or more can never survive generationally because family time is being sacrificed on the altar of ministry. The Church needs to not only promote commitment to Gospel ministry, but also promote commitment for quality family time if we are going to have strong marriages and keep our children in the faith.

The only exception to this is if a church also serves as a sort of half-way house for substance abusers or is a church community made up mostly of young singles. In those situations, a church needs to have continual meetings and services to meet the needs of their congregation, but they need to have enough staff to insure those ministering also have the necessary quality family time.

In my trans-local ministry, I have continually turned down many incredible opportunities to minister because they interfered with family vacation time or some other family-related event. I have learned that it is important to carve out family time before I fill my calendar with work and ministry-related events. There are about six weeks per year that I spend either with my wife or my whole family, and everything else on my schedule has to work around my quality family time.

I remember reading once where Hitler was arguing with an individual in Nazi Germany who said that he would never agree to the ideologies presented in the book, *Mein Kampf*. Hitler told him that didn't matter because the state was already brainwashing the next generation. The same thing is happening here in the United States as the public school system removes anything that has to do with God and replaces it with their worldly views of reality and life. Where do our children spend the majority of their time? Who are we allowing to influence the next generation of leaders?

God's intergenerational covenant brings deliverance:

> *And it came to pass in process of time, that the king of Egypt died: and the children of Israel sighed by reason of the bondage, and they cried, and their cry came up unto God by reason of the bondage. And God heard their groaning, and **God remembered His covenant with Abraham, with Isaac, and with Jacob. And God looked upon the children of Israel, and God had respect unto them*** (Exodus 2:23-25).

KEEPING FAITH IN THE JOURNEY

It wasn't just their groaning that got God's attention. It was the intergenerational covenant He had made with them that precipitated their mighty deliverance.

Why did God call Moses to be the deliverer? Most everybody in America would answer because of his courage, faith, and humility. Besides the fact that his mother was a very godly woman who refused to allow Pharaoh to kill him, we have to assume that there is a connection between Moses being chosen and the fact that he was a descendant of Levi, the tribe chosen to minister as priests.

Notice also in Exodus 4:13-14 that God chose Moses' biological brother Aaron, the Levite, to be his assistant, showing us again the generational importance of family in the Kingdom of God, which does encourage nepotism!

Once Moses and his brother Aaron returned to Egypt, Exodus chapters 5 through 11 record the devastating results of Pharaoh's refusal to allow God's people to leave. The Passover story depicted in Exodus 12:1-29 is actually "The Tale of Two Seeds." The godly seed of the Jews experienced a mighty deliverance that perpetuated the generational blessing of God while the ungodly seed came to an end because the firstborn son of every Egyptian family was killed by the destroying angel. The fact that God instructed the Jews to put the atoning blood on their doorpost to avoid the plague of the firstborn shows us that we can only have a generational blessing by applying the blood of Jesus to our families.

THE TEN COMMANDMENTS

From the Passover Story we move to the next historic event in the life of the nation of Israel, which is the receipt of the Ten Commandments. We will see God's generational emphasis in the instructions He gives us to receive blessing and to truly prosper in all that we do. The Ten Commandments are divided into two parts. The first four commandments have to do with our obligations to God. The next six have to do with our relationship with our fellow humanity.

The First and Second Commandments

As we study the Book of the Law, we find that anyone who broke one of the first three commandments was executed! We also see that a generational blessing or curse is attached to an individual and or a nation commensurate with their adherence to the Law of God revealed in God's first commandment.

> *And God spake all these words, saying, I am the Lord thy God, which have brought thee out of the land of Egypt, out of the house of bondage.* **Thou shalt have no other gods before Me. Thou shalt not make unto thee any graven image,** *or any likeness of any thing that is in heaven above, or that is in the earth beneath, or that is in the water under the earth: Thou shalt not bow down thyself to them, nor serve them: for I the Lord thy God am a jealous God,* **visiting the iniquity of the fathers upon the children unto the third and fourth generation of them that hate Me; And shewing mercy unto thousands of them that love Me, and keep My commandments** (Exodus 20:1-6).

As we examine the first commandment, we see that the worship of the one true God is the foundation of the law, without which there can be no generational blessing. Jesus reiterates this as the great commandment in Matthew 22:37-40. Generational blessings and curses are specifically attached to the second commandment. Whatever we do will, at minimum, influence three to four generations.

Romans 1:21-28 tells us how breaking this commandment leads to the sin of creature worship, in which homosexuality is one of the outcomes. Homosexuality is the ultimate anti-generation lifestyle!

Because that, when they knew God, they glorified Him not as God, neither were thankful; but became vain in their imaginations, and their foolish heart was darkened. Professing themselves to be wise, they became fools, and changed the glory of the uncorruptible God into an image made like to corruptible man, and to birds, and fourfooted beasts, and creeping things. Wherefore God also gave them up to uncleanness through the lusts of their own hearts, to dishonour their own bodies between themselves: who changed the truth of God into a lie, and worshipped and served the creature more than the Creator, who is blessed for ever. Amen. For this cause God gave them up unto vile affections: for even their women did change the natural use into that which is against nature: And likewise also the men, leaving the natural use of the woman, burned in their lust one toward another; men with men working that which is unseemly, and receiving in themselves that recompense of their error which was meet. And even as they did not like to retain God in their knowledge, God gave them over to a reprobate mind, to do those things which are not convenient (Romans 1:21-28).

The Third Commandment

Thou shalt not take the name of the Lord thy God in vain; for the Lord will not hold him guiltless that taketh His name in vain (Exodus 20:7).

Taking the Lord's name in vain or blasphemy carried with it the penalty of death! God honors, respects, and protects His name! Honoring His name in word and deed is the key to perpetuating a generational blessing in our families.

The Fourth Commandment

Remember the sabbath day, to keep it holy. Six days shalt thou labour, and do all thy work: But the seventh day is the sabbath of the Lord thy God: in it thou shalt not do any work, thou, nor thy son, nor thy daughter, thy manservant, nor thy maidservant, nor thy cattle, nor thy stranger that is within thy gates: For in six days the Lord made heaven and earth, the sea, and all that in them is, and rested the seventh day: wherefore the Lord blessed the sabbath day, and hallowed it (Exodus 20:8-11).

The Lord instituted the Sabbath day primarily as a sign between God and His people throughout their generations that He was going to take care of them if they took time away from work to focus their families on worshiping Him. We find a further explanation of this in Exodus 31:12-16.

And the Lord spake unto Moses, saying, Speak thou also unto the children of Israel, saying, Verily My sabbaths ye shall keep: for it is a sign between Me and you throughout your generations; that ye may know that I am the Lord that doth sanctify you. Ye shall keep the sabbath therefore; for it is holy unto you: every one that defileth it shall surely be put to death: for whosoever doeth any work therein, that soul shall be cut off from among his people. Six days may work be done; but in the seventh is the sabbath of rest, holy to the Lord: whosoever doeth any work in the sabbath day, he shall surely be put to death. Wherefore the children of Israel shall keep the sabbath, to observe the sabbath throughout their generations, for a perpetual covenant.

The Fifth Commandment

Honor thy father and thy mother: that thy days may be long upon the land which the Lord thy God giveth thee (Exodus 20:12).

These commandments were definitely given in the order of their importance. The question then arises, "Why would honoring your parents be more important than killing somebody?" The answer is found in the fifth commandment itself. When you live a life that dishonors godly parents, you are killing your past and your future because you are cutting off the generational blessing! The person who wants a good future must honor their godly past. Also, murder and adultery, the next two "thou shalt not" commandments are more likely to occur when we don't have a healthy relationship with our parents.

The Sixth Commandment

Thou shalt not kill (Exodus 20:13).

We have to realize that every time a person is murdered, a whole generational line is destroyed as well. Many of the problems England has had in the past 50 years in terms of remaining a world power can be directly related to all the millions of English men who were killed in World War II. I also believe there is a direct correlation between generational curses and abortion. Why? Abortion doesn't just stop a heart; it stops a lot of hearts!

The Seventh Commandment

Thou shalt not commit adultery (Exodus 20:14).

Why is adultery so grievous? It destroys the vehicle God uses to perpetuate His generational blessing—marriage (see Gen. 2:21-24). In marriage, two individual people become one flesh; in adultery, the one flesh divides again into two. The loyalty of the spouse committing adultery becomes divided between the paramour and the husband or wife. Adultery divides what God has joined. Satan's plan is to fragment the family so that God's plan of generational blessing through covenant is thwarted! God hates divorce because divorce means a broken family line.

Statistics show that 39 percent of those currently serving time in prison were brought up without their physical father at home most of the time.[1] Broken families usually bring broken lives and destroy the destiny of those who suffer the most—the children!

Does this mean that someone who commits adultery or who gets divorced has no chance of flowing in a generational blessing? No. God can redeem any situation and reverse a generational curse, but on the onset, adultery and divorce hurt Christian children as much as they hurt the children of those without Christ. Just ask the numerous broken families currently in the Body of Christ if their situation has negatively affected them.

The Eighth Commandment

Thou shalt not steal (Exodus 20:15).

In the context of Israel's culture, stealing here is also referring to taking something that was left to a person as part of their inheritance. Along these same lines, Proverbs 22:28 tells us not to move the ancient landmark.

One of the sins of America is the theft of what rightfully belongs to its hardworking citizens and their generations. When we instituted the income tax in 1913, it was the beginning of the road for our nation to fall into the lap of the Marxist Socialist belief system. This ungodly system says the state should own all property. This includes the children. They believe the state should educate and indoctrinate our children through publicly funded taxes. They endeavor to initiate a progressive tax policy to force the redistribution of wealth, including an outrageous inheritance tax that often robs our children of their financial and material inheritance. This is in direct contradiction to the Bible, which tells us that a good man leaves an inheritance to his children's children (see Prov. 13:22). It's another malicious attempt of the humanistic bent of the state to hinder the generational blessing.

The Ninth Commandment

> *Thou shalt not bear false witness against thy neighbor* (Exodus 20:16).

This is primarily dealing with lying about somebody in the Jewish court of law. A person falsely accused is in danger of losing his life, his freedom, or his property—all of which have much to do with perpetuating the generational blessing of God.

The Tenth Commandment

> *Thou shalt not covet thy neighbour's house, thou shalt not covet thy neighbour's wife, nor his manservant, nor his maidservant, nor his ox, nor his ass, nor any thing that is thy neighbour's* (Exodus 20:17).

God wants us to stay in our own lane. When we covet what someone else has, it is desiring a shortcut to obtain the blessing of God that a person has obtained by applying the laws of sowing and reaping.

GENERATIONAL PRIESTHOOD

As we complete our study of the generational emphasis in Exodus, we see that the priesthood established by God also contains a generational blessing.

And thou shalt gird them with girdles, Aaron and his sons, and put the bonnets on them: and the priest's office shall be theirs for a perpetual statute: and **thou shalt consecrate Aaron and his sons** (Exodus 29:9).

And thou shalt bring Aaron and his sons unto the door of the tabernacle of the congregation, and wash them with water. And thou shalt put upon Aaron the holy garments, and anoint him, and sanctify him; that he may minister unto me in the priest's office. And thou shalt bring his sons, and clothe them with coats: And thou shalt anoint them, as thou didst anoint their father, that they may minister unto me in the priest's office: **for their anointing shall surely be an everlasting priesthood throughout their generations** (Exodus 40:12-15).

One was not allowed to minister as a priest in the Levitical system if he was not a genealogical son of Levi and his father wasn't a priest before him. Not even Jesus was allowed to minister without the affirmation of His Father!

For every high priest taken from among men is ordained for men in things pertaining to God, that he may offer both gifts and sacrifices for sins: Who can have compassion on the ignorant, and on them that are out of the way; for that he himself also is compassed with infirmity. And by reason hereof he ought, as for the people, so also for himself, to offer for sins. And no man taketh this honour unto himself, but he that is called of God, as was Aaron. **So also Christ glorified not Himself to be made an high priest; but He that said unto Him, Thou art My Son, to day have I begotten Thee.** *As He saith also in another place,* **Thou art a priest for ever after the order of Melchisedec** (Hebrews 5:1-6).

It's sad to observe ministers call and appoint themselves to preach without any authorization from a local church or denomination. Many have even split their church and attempted to build a work with the members they stole from their mother church. Like Robert Duvall in the movie *The Apostle*, they ordain themselves, baptize themselves, and call themselves. They weren't sent; they just went!

Acts 13:1-4 gives us the biblical process for anointing and sending those to do the work of ministry; we should be sent by the Holy Spirit and affirmed by the local church.

> *Now there were in the church that was at Antioch certain prophets and teachers; as Barnabas, and Simeon that was called Niger, and Lucius of Cyrene, and Manaen, which had been brought up with Herod the tetrarch, and Saul. As they ministered to the Lord, and fasted, the Holy Ghost said, Separate Me Barnabas and Saul for the work whereunto I have called them. And when they had fasted and prayed, and laid their hands on them, they sent them away. So they, being sent forth by the Holy Ghost, departed...*

THINK ON THIS

People who allow economic reasons to stop them from believing God will provide for the amount of children He wants them to have are missing the miraculous provision that awaits all who obey.

What does Exodus 1:12 tell us was the result of the Egyptian persecution on Israel?

_____

_____

When we obey the purpose statement given to us in Genesis 1:28, we will _____ and be _____ in spite of all adversity!

It doesn't matter whether we live in the city or in a rough environment or in challenging economic times, God has already promised to bless us if we _____.

What is the primary plan of satan exposed in Exodus 1:15-22 and again in Exodus 10:8-11?

_____

_____

Which of the Ten Commandments given in Exodus chapter 20 deals with either generational blessings or curses?

_____

ENDNOTE

1. US Bureau of Justice Statistics, Survey of State Prison Inmates, 1991, page 9, located online at http://bjs.ojp.usdoj.gov/content/pub/pdf/SOSPI91.PDF.

CHAPTER 6

BEARERS OF THE GENERATIONAL VISION

This is a true saying, If a man desire the office of a bishop, he desireth a good work. A bishop then must be blameless, the husband of one wife, vigilant, sober, of good behaviour, given to hospitality, apt to teach; not given to wine, no striker, not greedy of filthy lucre; but patient, not a brawler, not covetous; one that ruleth well his own house, having his children in subjection with all gravity; (For if a man know not how to rule his own house, how shall he take care of the church of God?) (1 Timothy 3:1-5).

I can have great riches, success, celebrity status, great influence, as well as good physical health; but the greatest gift I have on earth is my family; it is the core of my strength, what I am primarily called to build, and my future voice that will allow me to speak long after my tent is folded up and I pass on to glory. —Joseph Mattera

IF we are to be bearers of the generational vision and blessing, we must realize God doesn't just do everything for us supernaturally. He has principles in place that He has instructed us to tap into that He promises will bring us success. Just as the enemy has a strategy to corrupt and defeat the people of God through generational curses, God has given us everything we need to participate in the divine nature and escape the corruption of the world caused by evil desires (see 2 Pet. 1:3-4). I believe that one of the reasons the Israelites were victorious in war was because of the unity of purpose and vision they had in their families throughout their generations.

GOD'S BATTLE STRATEGY

Once God had given the people of Israel His Ten Commandments, He began to prepare them to not only enter, but to conquer and possess their Promised Land. This group of wanderers was to be the bearer of God's generational covenant and would need to be able to do battle against the strategy of the enemy in the new land God had promised to not only this generation, but to their seed's seed.

> And the Lord spake unto Moses in the wilderness of Sinai, in the tabernacle of the congregation, on the first day of the second month, in the second year after they were come out of the land of Egypt, saying, Take ye the sum of all the congregation of the children of Israel, after their families, by the house of their fathers, with the number of their names, every male by their polls; from twenty years old and upward, all that are able to go forth to war in Israel: thou and Aaron shall number them by their armies. And with you there shall be a man of every tribe; every one head of the house of his fathers (Numbers 1:1-4).

> And Moses and Aaron took these men which are expressed by their names: And they assembled all the congregation together on the first day of the second month, and they declared their pedigrees

*after their families, by the house of their fathers, according to the number of the names, from twenty years old and upward, by their polls. As the Lord commanded Moses, so he numbered them in the wilderness of Sinai. And the children of Reuben, Israel's eldest son, by their generations, after their families, by the house of their fathers, according to the number of the names, by their polls, every male from twenty years old and upward, **all that were able to go forth to war** (Numbers 1:17-20).*

The American Church plans to win back the nation with one prayer event or strategy. The enemy had a strategy that took more than 300 years from the time of the arrival of the Mayflower on the shores of Cape Cod in 1609 to bring this nation into the present humanistic culture. We have so many conferences on "Taking Our Cities for God" and "How to do Spiritual Warfare," but if we don't understand God's principles for preparing for war, we will never win! These passages show that spiritual warfare primarily involves getting our families in order as preparation for the life-and-death battles we will have in the worldly culture we are called to conquer.

Most new believers are first-generation Christians with a large percentage of them coming from broken families and bad marriages. Because the enemy's strategy has been to destroy generational blessings, they are not prepared for the intense spiritual warfare manifest in the pressures of daily life, causing a large percentage of new believers to fall away after a short period of time.

A salient point that speaks to us in this chapter of Numbers is how this army lined up in preparation for battle. They came together to battle based on their families and on the leadership of the heads of households. Their qualification for the army was based on proving their pedigree or their birthright. They came against the enemy based on the corporate anointing of their generations, their families, and the house of their fathers.

No wonder the Church is getting defeated in the cultural war! While we declare our victory over the devil in spiritual warfare conferences, our marriages are falling apart with a rampant divorce rate, our kids are non-committal to the cause of Christ, and while female attendance is at an all-time high, male attendance continues to drop. In many churches, male attendance makes up a paltry 10-15 percent of the congregation. While many ministers are praying for revival, I say we'd better get the foundations right, or all our experiences with God will be short lived!

THE CRISIS OF MALE HEADSHIP

We need to begin in the area of leadership of the heads of households. The last time I checked, Ephesians 5:23 still teaches that the husband is the head of the wife, even as Christ is the head of the Church. My heart goes out to Christian single moms who try to nurture boys in the faith. It is very difficult for them without a strong father figure living with them in the home as a committed marriage partner.

Although I believe in and release women in ministry, by far the biggest challenge we have in the inner city churches is the absence of male church attendees and leadership.

It is essential for us to get the heads of families involved with us before we can successfully win a war. As the family goes, so goes the Church! As a Church, we would do well to face this current crisis of male headship! Unless, of course, we desire only a single generation impact. Most recent revivals didn't even last a decade. I am not criticizing; any move of God is better than having no move of God! But I believe God would have us tap into His battle strategies and broaden our vision to impact not only this generation, but generations to come!

It is my experience that when the father of a Christian home serves the Lord and is faithfully involved in a local church, there is an 85 percent chance that the rest of the family, including all the children, will also serve the Lord and be involved in the same church. Conversely, when just the mother of the family attends church, there is only a 15 percent chance the rest of the family will do likewise!

WHAT IS YOUR FAMILY BANNER?

In recent years, it has become popular for individuals and corporations to come up with a mission statement. Even many churches have developed these for the sake of focusing the members of the congregation. However, I believe we also have to realize that, since the Church is a "family of families" and each distinct family has its own history and generations, it will take all of the families and their generational blessings converging on our communities, cities, and nations to make a difference.

In Numbers chapter 2, God instructs the Israelites to arrange their tribal camps around the Tent of the Meeting, or the tabernacle, under their family's standard, or family banner. Some countries call this the family coat of arms.

> And the Lord spake unto Moses and unto Aaron, saying, Every man of the children of Israel shall pitch **by his own standard, with the ensign of their father's house:** far off about **the tabernacle** of the congregation shall they pitch. ... And the children of Israel did according to all that the Lord commanded Moses: so they pitched by their standards, and so they set forward, every one after their families, according to the house of their fathers (Numbers 2:1-2,34).

Each family had their own purpose and destiny, which the banner or ensign reflected, yet they were in complete harmony with what God was orchestrating with Israel as a whole.

Jewish writers say the standards of the Hebrew tribes were symbols borrowed from the prophetic blessing of Jacob—Judah's being a lion,

Benjamin's a wolf, and so forth—and the ensigns, or banners, were distinguished by their colors. The colors of each tribe were the same as the precious stone representing that tribe in the breastplate of the High Priest.[1] It is interesting that we even see the generational proclamations of Jacob over his sons reflected in their family banners. Do you know what your family banner is to represent?

The arrangement of the family camps around the tabernacle, the Tent of Meeting, the Church, shows the balance God desired between the tribes and the Church. Our families should never be neglected for the Church, but conversely, we should never neglect the Church for our families! They are not one against the other, but should be understood in the context of a family of families functioning together for the Kingdom and glory of God.

God doesn't want us to sacrifice our uniqueness as an individual or a family, yet He wants us to sacrifice our independence for the purpose of interdependently relating to one another as the community of Christ! The Bible never said to seek first the family or the Church, but the Kingdom of God (see Matt. 6:33). When we do this, we will never neglect the family or the Church because both are included in the Kingdom.

We need to function together in unity without sacrificing our distinctions, because true unity is never uniformity, but a convergence of divergent entities so that we can truly reflect oneness in the Body of Christ. Imagine the power that will be released in the Body of Christ when we understand that, as we come together in church, we are not only coming together as individuals, but as families with the explosive power of our generational standards and blessings! When individuals, healthy families, and heads of families come together as the Body of Christ to obey the Word of God, cultural and religious strongholds holding communities captive will be shattered!

Of course, in the humanistic culture we have been raised in and exposed to, it is very difficult to establish healthy family habits. Often first generation believers need time to unlearn the negative traits they received from their dysfunctional family backgrounds and learn to deal with the generational curses passed down to them from previous generations. It may not be until the second generation of believers that truly healthy family habits are established and entrenched. It takes a lot of work to get a generation to function correctly, but the Bible teaches us the consequences of the failure of a generation to seek first the Kingdom of God.

THE FAILURE OF A GENERATION

The Bible teaches us that whole generations can be distinguished by a particular thing, and they can either fail or succeed based on how they deal with the issue or challenge of their day. Proverbs 30:11-14 describes what such a generation might look like even today:

> There is a generation that curseth their father, and doth not bless their mother. There is a generation that are pure in their own eyes, and yet is not washed from their filthiness. There is a generation, O how lofty are their eyes! and their eyelids are lifted up. There is a generation, whose teeth are as swords, and their jaw teeth as knives, to devour the poor from off the earth, and the needy from among men.

In Numbers 13:1-3 we see Moses sending out heads of the children of Israel to spy out the land they were called to conquer:

> And the Lord spake unto Moses, saying, Send thou men, that they may search the land of Canaan, which I give unto the children of Israel: of every tribe of their fathers shall ye send a man, every one a ruler among them. And Moses by the commandment of the Lord sent them from the wilderness of Paran: all those men were heads of the children of Israel.

Instead of believing God, 10 of the 12 spies brought back an evil report in which they showed more faith in the giants of the land of Canaan to defeat them than in the God of Abraham, Isaac, and Jacob to deliver them! Their evil report spread throughout the whole camp of the children of Israel and caused the people to begin to murmur against Moses and Aaron.

> *And all the congregation lifted up their voice, and cried; and the people wept that night. And all the children of Israel murmured against Moses and against Aaron: and the whole congregation said unto them, Would God that we had died in the land of Egypt! or would God we had died in this wilderness! And wherefore hath the Lord brought us unto this land, to fall by the sword, that our wives and our children should be a prey? were it not better for us to return into Egypt? And they said one to another, Let us make a captain, and let us return into Egypt* (Numbers 14:1-4).

God responded to this national show of unbelief in Numbers 14:11-12 by saying He was going to disinherit them:

> *And the Lord said unto Moses, How long will this people provoke Me? and how long will it be ere they believe Me, for all the signs which I have showed among them? I will smite them with the pestilence, and disinherit them, and will make of thee a greater nation and mightier than they.*

Imagine, not only individual souls can miss the calling of God; a whole generation can as well! These passages in Numbers 14:26-31 show that God will bypass one generation and pass their destiny on to the next generation!

> *And the Lord spake unto Moses and unto Aaron, saying, How long shall I bear with this evil congregation, which murmur against Me? I have heard the murmurings of the children*

of Israel, which they murmur against Me. Say unto them, As truly as I live, saith the Lord, as ye have spoken in Mine ears, so will I do to you: Your carcasses shall fall in this wilderness; and all that were numbered of you, according to your whole number, from twenty years old and upward, which have murmured against Me, Doubtless ye shall not come into the land, concerning which I sware to make you dwell therein, save Caleb the son of Jephunneh, and Joshua the son of Nun. But your little ones, which ye said should be a prey, them will I bring in, and they shall know the land which ye have despised (Numbers 14:26-31).

THE JEWISH GENERATION
DURING THE TIME OF CHRIST

A whole generation of Jews during the time of Christ missed their destiny in God as well. We read the words of Jesus speaking judgment upon a whole generation in Matthew 24:34-35, *"Verily I say unto you, this generation shall not pass, till all these things be fulfilled. Heaven and earth shall pass away, but My words shall not pass away."*

Jesus was so troubled by this, He wept over the city of Jerusalem.

And when He was come near, He beheld the city, and wept over it, saying, If thou hadst known, even thou, at least in this thy day, the things which belong unto thy peace! but now they are hid from thine eyes. For the days shall come upon thee, that thine enemies shall cast a trench about thee, and compass thee round, and keep thee in on every side, and shall lay thee even with the ground, and thy children within thee; and they shall not leave in thee one stone upon another; because thou knewest not the time of thy visitation (Luke 19:41-44).

In the 1960s, the United States went through a very turbulent time that many refer to as the sexual or cultural revolution. With rock groups like the Beatles appearing on the scene—espousing rebellion, free love, and drugs—a whole generation of young people rebelled against authority and espoused a lifestyle that came to be known as the hippie movement. Many of these were influenced by New Age gurus, Eastern mysticism, and the radical left teachings of Marxist revolutionaries, and they grew up to make up the majority of our current crop of elite university professors and left-wing politicians.

At the same time, the Jesus Movement took place in California and swept through the whole nation, which resulted in thousands of young people coming to Christ. Simultaneously, a great Charismatic renewal shook the Roman Catholic and mainline Protestant denominations, and thousands of nominal Christians renewed their faith and were filled with the Holy Spirit! While it appeared a whole generation of young people would be lost to the world, the Lord raised up an incredible standard that successfully countered the plan of satan to brainwash the minds of a whole nation. God always has a plan of continuity to perpetuate His Kingdom from one generation to the next!

One of the most important things in the local church is to plan for the next generation. Unfortunately, it is a rare thing when a local church builds upon the success of its founding generation, because there is little or no proper planning for leadership transition and succession. Fortunately, God has given us His plan for successfully passing the baton of leadership on to the next generation.

PASSING THE BATON

In Numbers 27:12-23, we read how Moses was able to pass the vision God gave him for the nation of Israel on to his faithful servant Joshua. The lessons learned in this narrative cannot be overstated. Many pastors and Christian leaders who do not have a proper succession plan in which they intentionally process leaders to take their place can learn much from this passage of Scripture.

> And the Lord said unto Moses, Get thee up into this mount Abarim, and see the land which I have given unto the children of Israel. And when thou hast seen it, thou also shalt be gathered unto thy people, as Aaron thy brother was gathered. For ye rebelled against My commandment in the desert of Zin, in the strife of the congregation, to sanctify Me at the water before their eyes: that is the water of Meribah in Kadesh in the wilderness of Zin (Numbers 27:12-14).

Moses asked the Lord to reveal to him God's choice for his successor.

> And Moses spake unto the Lord, saying, Let the Lord, the God of the spirits of all flesh, set a man over the congregation, which may go out before them, and which may go in before them, and which may lead them out, and which may bring them in; that the congregation of the Lord be not as sheep which have no shepherd (Numbers 27:15-17).

God will never leave His sheep without a shepherd. As Christian leaders, we need to realize this and begin to prepare and train the one that God has already chosen to succeed us in the guidance and leadership of His people.

> And the Lord said unto Moses, Take thee Joshua the son of Nun, a man in whom is the spirit, and lay thine hand upon him; And set him before Eleazar the priest, and before all the congregation; and give him a charge in their sight. And thou shalt put some of thine honour upon him, that all the congregation of the children of Israel may be obedient. And he shall stand before Eleazar the priest, who shall ask counsel for him after the judgment of Urim before the Lord: at his word

shall they go out, and at his word they shall come in, both he, and all the children of Israel with him, even all the congregation. And Moses did as the Lord commanded him: and he took Joshua, and set him before Eleazar the priest, and before all the congregation: And he laid his hands upon him, and gave him a charge, as the Lord commanded by the hand of Moses (Numbers 27:18-23).

After doing all that the Lord commanded, Moses was ready to pass on to glory. It is unfortunate that this has not become the model most churches follow. Too often a pastor goes on to be with the Lord or is removed from ministry, and a person totally unqualified or without the vision and call to lead that congregation becomes the pastor, and the work of God begins to go downhill.

In our local church, we are ever mindful of preparing for the next generation of leadership. Half of our strong leaders are in their mid-40s and early 50s, and the other half are 30 years old and under. It is in balance that we are planning for our local church to be successful for generations to come! I don't want to wait until I am in my late 60s to figure out a succession plan.

THINK ON THIS

Each family or tribe had their own purpose and destiny, which the banner or ensign reflected, yet they were in complete harmony with what God was orchestrating with Israel as a whole. Jewish writers say the standards of the Hebrew tribes were symbols borrowed from the prophetic blessing of Jacob as described in Genesis 49:3-23, Judah's being a lion and Benjamin's a wolf.

What is the standard or the coat of arms for your family?

_____

_____

What does it stand for?

_____

_____

In Numbers 14:11-31, what happened to ten men and their families who returned from spying out the land in Canaan and gave Moses and Aaron a bad report?

_____

_____

_____

_____

Read Matthew chapter 24. What was Jesus speaking about in Matthew 24:34?

_____

_____

_____

_____

One of the most important things in the local church is to:

_____

WALK IN GENERATIONAL BLESSINGS

What did Moses ask God for in Numbers 27:15-17?

_____

_____

Why?

_____

_____

Are you a leader or a pastor? _____ Have you begun
to seek God for your successor? _____ What do you
need to do once God reveals this person to you?

ENDNOTE

1. Robert Jamieson, *A Critical and Explanatory Commentary of the
   Old and New Testaments* (Memphis, TN: General Books, 2010);
   see also Genesis 49:3-23 and Exodus 28:17-21.

CHAPTER 7

PERPETUATION OF
THE COVENANT

by Justin Mattera

"HOMEGROWN" just doesn't work anymore. It's really sad. Churchgoers and pastors are losing their kids by the droves. Children are either getting "re-saved" by some other person or ministry or are losing their salvation altogether. It's a phenomenon that makes you wonder what we are doing when the Bible puts so much emphasis on generational continuity (i.e., Abraham, Isaac, and Jacob; the God of our forefathers, visiting sin up to three generations, and so forth).

How could we have possibly gone so astray as to lose one of the basic tenets of our faith? But not just that, it seems as if we aren't even doing anything about it. Continually I see parents just left praying for their children once the children decide Jesus isn't for them, instead of taking precautionary steps to prevent the disaster in the first place. This is a problem that requires a preventative solution, not a reactionary one.

THE FOUR KILLERS

I believe there are four main causes for the lack of continuity between generations: intellectual; emotional dysfunction; lack of leadership opportunity; and, non-thriving communities (youth groups).

1. Intellectual

Intellectual losses are staggering. Sadly, the first time most Christian kids hear a reasonable explanation for the universe is when they are in college. Sometimes, but not as frequently, this happens in high school.

The strategic onslaught to a biblical worldview on college campuses leaves one with a Darwinian perspective on life and the Bible. Only the strong survive.

I have seen Christian kids befuddled by some of the stupidest arguments known to humanity. Arguments like, "God is your mother," or better yet, "Genesis is a nice big poem." Why does this happen? It happens because they have walked into a college campus with absolutely no intellectual background or teaching on basic philosophy, politics, economics, and science.

The first time they hear a rational understanding of the world and how it works is usually from a hyper-liberal, evolutionary atheist.

Even if they don't lose their salvation, usually they will be corrupted forever. This is because they will begin to read the Bible through a hyper-liberal, evolutionary, atheistic lens. Which, I would say, is just as bad as becoming an atheist. It does just as much harm to God's Word.

In our youth group, I take all the graduating high school students and give them a three-hour lesson on God, politics, and the universe. Then I point them to good reading material, and when the onslaught happens, at least they are prepared, know it is coming, and know where to turn.

2. Emotional Dysfunction

This is an interesting topic that is rarely talked about. Yes, your dysfunction and poor emotional health cause your kids to be turned off from the Gospel. Working as a youth leader, I see it happen all the time.

"Justin, why do my parents scream at me all the time?"

"Justin, why are my parents throwing my sin in my face?"

"Justin, why are my parents separated?"

Those are just some of the questions I get on a daily basis. The sad reality is dysfunction has become the norm in the Christian household. And since such dysfunction is directly contrary to the Gospel, for good reason it turns kids off from God.

There are the detached parents who never give their kids a father. There are the irate parents who love Jesus in church. There are the emotionally non-existent parents because ministry always comes first. And there are the parents who never dealt with whatever emotional dysfunction ailed them as kids, and therefore, pass it on to their children. And trust me on this one—as much as you try to hide the struggles you had since childhood, if you did not take care of them, your kids will have them.

On a side note, the amount of surrogate fatherhood that needs to take place with kids who actually have a dad who attends the church is pathetic and speaks to a more overarching need for men to man up and be fathers.

3. Lack of Leadership Opportunity

Two essentials for young people are trust and something to put abnormally high amounts of energy into. When a young person has no opportunities to lead, both those factors are missing.

Distrust goes beyond just words and always asking your kid, "Where were you, and who were you with?" It is inherent in what you allow them to do or lead. Of course, don't allow a 15-year-old to run the sound ministry. But how about organizing the schedule in the sound team or heading up its recruiting?

Underestimating the potential of a young person can be deadly. Deadly for them. They will turn to other communities who value their potential. Sadly these communities turn out to be mostly college professors or school clubs that sidetrack them from their faith.

Then there is that intense level of passion in young people. If this passion isn't harnessed for something good, who knows what it will be spent on? Here's what: bad relationships, hating parents, and putting their passion somewhere outside the church. Find small things you can trust your young people with, and as they prove responsible, allow that list of things to grow.

4. Non-thriving Communities (Youth Groups)

When I was younger, I knew that some youth groups were places where I could go to "hook up" with people, or find drugs and satisfy other fleshly desires a 15-year-old might have. Thankfully my parents never let me attend other youth groups. The more I travel and the more I encounter young people, the more I see the huge lack of thriving youth groups. Most have become safe havens for sin.

But that is the worst-case scenario. There are other kinds of shortcoming as well. One is that there are literally no youth groups at all. Therefore, there is no place to connect with other like-minded, God-hungry teenagers. Another issue is the youth group that has been relegated to some older person who believes they were called to youth ministry, but has no clue as to how to actually relate with them. They may love the kids, but ask any of the youth and you'll find that youth group is a laborious affair.

A red-hot youth group helps young people stay plugged into Christ and provides productive relationships, not to mention helps them transition into a healthy adult life in the church.

MY STORY

A quick understanding of my personal story will help illustrate my later main points for developing generational continuity based on the situational leadership approach.

My younger years (up until age 10) were full of directives. My parents did not ask me when I wanted to go to sleep. They told me when I was going to go to sleep; they regulated who my friends were. They told me when I was allowed to be outside of the house. They gave me clear rules on when the television was allowed to be on and when it had to be off. During these years, I formed a perspective on how to live a good life. Whether I was to follow this model or not is a different story, but at least I now had one to refer to.

The next stage of my life (11-17) is usually a parent's most dreaded years, adolescence. During these years, my memory is full of books my dad sold to me. (Meaning he constantly tried to sell or pitch books to me that would be beneficial or helpful for me to read.) Also, my parents encouraged me to give generously to the church as I got my first job. And they encouraged me to join a ministry in the church as I matured.

Their guidance helped shape my life. They prodded me in the direction they knew was best for me. They helped me understand why those decisions were good ones and did not just say I had to do them. Because of this, I read all of John Maxwell's leadership series by the age of 12. In eighth grade, I joined my church's sound team and later became a lead technician. At 16, I joined the youth staff and fell in love with leading others to deeper relationships with Christ.

My parents had successfully directed me to understanding a great model for living. Then they guided me in making better choices on my own. Next came their support for decisions I would make. They had to trust that I learned from them and that I was ready to make some big choices myself.

That first big choice was taking a year off from college to go live with my uncle in Ohio. It was not the decision they'd hoped for. But I decided I needed to get away for a year to sort things out before I could go on to college. And my uncle just so happened to be starting up a Bible school. Needless to say, it was the best, and first, decision I ever made with my life.

After that year, I enrolled in Baruch College in New York City. It's a business college. I wanted to pursue a greater understanding of how money works, management, and business models. There I found InterVarsity Christian Fellowship and decided to work with them full-time. Sophomore year I had a discussion with my parents that I would be working with them full-time on campus as chapter president. That meant me really pulling back on my duties in the church. They supported it, and again, it paid off.

My next and current stage in life came after that year in InterVarsity. My parents saw how I had grown and were now ready to give me a crack at leadership. When I was 20, the previous youth director and my parents felt it was time I take the reins and begin to lead our church's youth and young adults' ministry.

SITUATIONAL LEADERSHIP— A PARENTING MODEL

Situational leadership is a well-known management model that corporations and leaders use everywhere. I learned these principles and found them very applicable to discipleship and parenting.

There are four stages in situational leadership:

1. Directing

2. Guiding

3. Supporting

4. Delegating

Each stage represents a bracket an employee, disciple, or in this case, your child, will go through under your leadership. Going through my own life stages under my parents' leadership will help illustrate each stage. After that I will discuss some basic roadblocks to generational continuity.

Directing

Have you ever been in a supermarket and saw a parent interacting with a child? Or more correctly put, a child calling the shots with the parents, and thought something along the lines of, *Wow, if that were my child I would set him straight*. If so, you have directing down pat.

You're not your 2-year-old's best friend. You are teaching her right from wrong, good from bad. And in the process, you are training her how to not be selfish all the time.

When I was young, my parents did not ask me when I wanted to go to bed. They gave me a bedtime and made sure I followed it. When I did something wrong, they did not think I would inherently realize, know punishment was good, and therefore not lie about it and be honest. They knew I was born a liar and so dealt with me accordingly.

The directing phase is full of just that: directives. Parents are the bosses, and what they say goes. No matter how many tantrums, tears, and screams, parents know what's best. My parents made sure my television viewing was regulated. They made sure I was reading books and doing homework before I hung out with friends. School nights were never times for me to be with anyone but the family and my schoolwork. Sleepovers, no matter how much I begged, weren't allowed at the same rate my friends had them. This went on until around the age of 10.

Guiding

Thankfully, directing doesn't last forever. There is a point when you start to move away from breathing down someone's neck, trust what you taught him or her, and guide that person toward the right way. This time develops relationship. You still know what is best. But instead of directing, you switch to guiding. You are not handing down laws. Instead, you explain and show why those laws are there and how they are helpful.

This stage for me was from about 11 to 17. My parents no longer told me what books to read. They constantly showed me good books and told me why they would be good to read. From there I would pick them up and fall in love myself. They taught me that serving in ministry was one of the greatest things I could do. So I joined the sound team, and they celebrated that decision.

When it seemed like I was losing focus and going off track, they had conversations with me that pushed me back in the right direction. They helped inspire self-motivated improvement. Granted, it didn't always work. I still had to figure out who I was. I was still a liar, and I was still full of sin. But thankfully, in the process, they never reverted back to directives. That would have made me hate them and become that stereotypical, rebellious teenager.

But I knew the right way. And more importantly, I understood why it was right. However, no matter how useful I was told homework was for my grades and character, I still never did it. When guiding someone, even though you want them to be perfect in every area, remember how flawed you are as well, and give that person, or child, room to grow.

Supporting

Supporting is sometimes the hardest thing to do. It's keeping that smile on your face when someone tells you they want to do something crazy and pretending like you're OK with it. That's what my parents did, sort of, when I told them I was off to Ohio for a year and not going to start college right away. It was a big move and meant they had to put a lot of trust in my reasoning.

I graduated with a class of over 950. Each of them had a college they were attending after graduation (I went to a specialized school). Each one, except me, that is. Next to Justin's name was N/A. Boy that was fun to explain.

But guess what? At age 17 this was the first major decision I was making with my life. I knew before I went to college God was calling me to spend a year with Him and become grounded in my faith. So I shipped myself off to live with my uncle Lenny Weston in Ohio for a year to attend his newly opened Bible school. Needless to say, it was the best decision I ever made in my life. Who knows where I would be now if I did not become grounded in God before I went to college.

My parents had to trust in the instruction they had given me over the past 17 years. They had to trust that they taught me well and now it was time for me to begin to take the reins. They supported me, counseled me, and trusted me. Even though it didn't make much sense and they had legitimate concerns, they knew they had raised me right.

When I went to college a year later, they again supported me to join InterVarsity. I took some time off from heavy ministry work in the church to grow in my leadership ability on my college campus. Again, it was a decision that paid off well.

Delegating

This is where the big guns of parenting came out.

Letting go.

For 20 years my mother and father discipled me, trained me, counseled me, and loved me. Now it was time to see what I could do.

After some prayer and discussion, Kristian Hernandez (the former youth director of eight years) and my parents (senior pastors) decided to allow me to lead the youth group. For some parents, it wouldn't be such an obvious form of delegation as giving your child a youth ministry.

Delegation in the form of parenting is trusting that you taught them well. Then it's handing over leadership of their lives to them. It means telling them they are now men or women and initiating them into becoming responsible for their lives. Sadly, for most kids, this either never happens or happens way too young.

Delegating is handing over responsibility. It's no longer micromanaging. It's no longer thinking your input is required. It's no longer thinking adult and child. You are bringing another adult into the world. And if you don't think your son or daughter is ever ready to be an adult, then that means you are saying you never raised your child to be one. It means you never taught your child how to make good decisions or how to say yes and no to things properly. It means you doubt your own ability to raise the truest of true disciples, your child.

The reason for the strong tone is this—switching from being the only adult who knows what's best to having two adults who make their own decisions is very difficult. But if it's not being done, you have to understand what that means—at the core, you do not believe that you raised a sufficient child. Every kid needs to feel accepted as an adult first by his or her parents.

As a youth director, I enjoy a lot of freedom. That inherently speaks to the trust my parents have in a) how I was raised, b) the experiences that shaped me, and c) the judgment I have as a man. But there are some monsters that try to creep in when raising up the next generation. Let's take a look at them.

ROADBLOCKS

Raising the next generation is not easy by any means. And with it come some inherent roadblocks. Knowing what they are can help you better make decisions when running into them. Some are warnings of what lies ahead, so remember them when you're making decisions.

Biological Versus Spiritual

When you have spiritual sons or daughters, you help them grow. Part of that is allowing them to fail so that they can learn. Even though letting people fail is a concrete leadership concept, putting that to practice with biological children is hard. We want them to be perfect in every way. We don't want to see them fail because it hurts us more. Sometimes when they fail, we feel it reflects on us.

It's a hard decision to make. And where the line is drawn is also hard to distinguish. How far do you let them fall before you pick them back up? Do you trust that God is ultimately taking care of their souls?

There are tough questions to ask. In the end though, it has to be done. If we never let our children make mistakes, then we either drive them crazy by shoving our advice down their throats day and night, or they never learn to cope with one of the most important lessons in life, which is failure.

I encourage you to reflect on the differences in how you lead your spiritual children and your biological children. Then note the differences in how each child (spiritual and biological) responds to you as a whole.

Directing Forever, Delegating From the Start

Here are the two most common problems I have seen: parents who never stop ordering their kids around and parents who start delegating from day one.

First there are the incessant directors, the bosses. Their children can never be adults in those parents' eyes. They feel the need to constantly bombard their children with what they think their children should do. This manifests itself in the college student who is still only majoring in something because their parents said to or in the children who are 20 and above and still have to give an hourly report of their lives.

Some children walk away from the faith despite having had great parents; I've seen it happen. But even if that does happen, that doesn't mean their parents should revert to trying to control their lives.

When children need to move halfway across the nation to dorm at a college in order to get away from their overbearing parents, there is a problem. Or if children still feel the need to lie about what they are doing when they are 25, alarms should be going off. Even if they're wrong, shoving it in their faces isn't going to help. And it sure won't do wonders for your future relationship.

Then there are the parents who delegated since the day the baby came out of the womb. Kid wants to watch a movie, kid gets to do it. Kid wants to sleep over at a friend's house, kid gets to do it. Kid doesn't want to do any schoolwork, kid gets to not do it. These are the younger years when parents try to be friends to their children instead of directing them on how to be proper human beings. This kind of parenting produces selfish, lazy, unproductive citizens in society. They're the ones who never grow up or who think they are adults at age 12 or 15. "Spare the rod, spoil the child" is a great testament for a directing parent during the beginning years of childhood.

Can She Trust You? Can You Trust Him?

The ugly *trust* word. We touched on this a little before when we talked about delegating. Trust is the essential element that is built up over the years a child is growing up. It can easily be ripped apart. But usually if there are trust problems later on, it means trust was never built to begin with.

If you cannot trust your child to become an adult, here is what it means—you don't trust your own parenting ability. If your children cannot trust you to love them, to let them fail, and to support them, then here is what it means—they feel you are trying to control them.

Hear my love in all of these harsh statements. Your children will become adults. That is a biological fact. Their minds will start changing at a certain age. They will begin to look different. They will begin to process information differently. And if they don't perceive you seeing that in them (whether they are serving God or not), then they will run the other way.

Usually, the parents who disciple well learn to trust their children and go through the cycle of situational leadership (either deliberately or unknowingly) will have children who grow up to love Jesus with all their hearts.

Some won't, but that is a sad exception. The present reality is most of our kids are not growing up and staying in the faith, so we need better biological discipleship.

To conclude, here are a couple of points to remember:

- *Above all, children want honesty.* If you have character flaws, they know it. Don't act like you are perfect. Readily admit when you are wrong, and grow in allowing God to work on your heart. Allow your kids to see that you're working at changing and becoming more like Christ.

- *Young leaders desire trust and encouragement.* Give them responsibility and trust them to do it, even if it seems they are going about it in a different way than you would. See what happens after the deadline for the finished product and grow them from there. If you cannot see them doing it on their own, give them something you do see them doing on their own.

- *Rebuke when necessary; show commitment and love always.* Don't beat around the bush or hold back for the sake of their feelings. Young people love directness. You will be surprised how well they respond to rebuke if they know you are committed to their success and show that you love them.

- *Actions speak loud—include them.* Bring them to leadership meetings. Show them the ropes. Take them with you on business or ministry trips. They will never forget those moments when they grow up.

- *This is a Kingdom-wide call, not just for pastors.* The rate at which the Church is losing its children to the world is astonishing. There needs to be change in how we raise our kids.

THINK ON THIS

The four main reasons why we are currently losing our young people are:

1. _____

2. _____

3. _____

4. _____

Telling someone what to do is the _____ stage and is done for young kids or newly hired employees.

When a child reaches the stage of knowing best and being able to make decisions for themselves, it is called the _____ stage.

The two main stages parents tend to focus on, and that therefore often become roadblocks, are the _____ and _____ stages.

What do your children want above all else when it comes to your shortcomings and failures?

_____

_____

_____

_____

For rebuke to be effective to young people, they need to know you are _____ to them.

The four stages of Situation Leadership are (add a brief description):

1._____

_____

2._____

_____

3._____

_____

4._____

_____

CHAPTER 8

WANTED: GODLY LEADERSHIP IN THE HOME

Give up money, give up fame, give up science, give the earth itself and all it contains rather than do an immoral act. And never suppose that in any possible situation, or under any circumstances, it is best for you to do a dishonorable thing, however slightly so it may appear to you. ...From the practice of the purest virtue, you may be assured you will derive the most sublime comforts in every moment of life, and in the moment of death. —Thomas Jefferson, 1785[1]

THE FOLLY OF ACHAN'S SIN

JOSHUA 7:13-18 uncovers the folly of Achan's sin and shows how God respected the family lineage of a person before He dealt with him in judgment! The Lord used a protocol in which He went through the heads of each level of leadership in Israel; by tribes, families, heads of households, and then to the individual who sinned.

> *Up, sanctify the people, and say, Sanctify yourselves against to morrow: for thus saith the Lord God of Israel, There is an*

accursed thing in the midst of thee, O Israel: thou canst not stand before thine enemies, until ye take away the accursed thing from among you. In the morning therefore ye shall be brought according to your tribes: and it shall be, that the tribe which the Lord taketh shall come according to the families thereof; and the family which the Lord shall take shall come by households; and the household which the Lord shall take shall come man by man. And it shall be, that he that is taken with the accursed thing shall be burnt with fire, he and all that he hath: because he hath transgressed the covenant of the Lord, and because he hath wrought folly in Israel **So Joshua rose up early in the morning, and brought Israel by their tribes; and the tribe of Judah was taken: And he brought the family of Judah; and he took the family of the Zarhites: and he brought the family of the Zarhites man by man; and Zabdi was taken: And he brought his household man by man; and Achan, the son of Carmi, the son of Zabdi, the son of Zerah, of the tribe of Judah, was taken** (Joshua 7:13-18).

Everything in the Kingdom of God starts and ends with the heads of households and families. My wife and I have always felt the great weight of this burden. We always connect our destiny and our spirituality with the real condition of our marriage and children. With our busy schedules, spending the proper amount of time with our children has always been a big challenge. I got up by 6:30 A.M. and often made breakfast for my children and read and prayed with them. I would not only use the Scriptures, but also books dealing with youth. Then I would drive them all to school and continue to pray with them, ensuring I would spend quality time with them and have a profound influence on their lives each and every day.

If you don't know what kinds of materials to use in teaching your children, there are many resources available from ministries such as Focus on the Family and Josh McDowell; even old materials used as a catechism for children can give a lot of aid. Of course, the greatest resource you have in terms of teaching your children is the Scriptures themselves. With young adults, the Book of Proverbs is especially helpful. The responsibility for parents to nurture their children in the ways of the Lord is so great—its importance cannot be overstated!

THE BIBLICAL MANDATE
TO TRAIN UP OUR CHILDREN

One of the most powerful passages dealing with the biblical mandate to train up our children and maintain a godly household is found in Deuteronomy 6:1-9:

> *Now these are the commandments, the statutes, and the judgments, which the Lord your God commanded to teach you, that ye might do them in the land whither ye go to possess it:* **That thou mightest fear the Lord thy God, to keep all His statutes and His commandments, which I command thee, thou, and thy son, and thy son's son, all the days of thy life; and that thy days may be prolonged.** *Hear therefore, O Israel, and observe to do it; that it may be well with thee, and that ye may increase mightily, as the Lord God of thy fathers hath promised thee, in the land that floweth with milk and honey. Hear, O Israel: The Lord our God is one Lord: And thou shalt love the Lord thy God with all thine heart, and with all thy soul, and with all thy might. And these words, which I command thee this day, shall be in thine heart:* **And thou shalt teach them diligently unto thy children, and shalt talk of them when thou sittest in thine house, and when thou walkest by the way, and when thou liest down, and when thou risest up. And thou shalt bind them for a sign upon thine hand, and they shall be as frontlets between**

thine eyes. And thou shalt write them upon the posts of thy house, and on thy gates (Deuteronomy 6:1-9).

As you can see, the discipling of children involves not only Bible instruction; it is to be a way of life for the godly family. Allow life itself to give you the opportunities to instruct your children and family in such subjects as how to use your time and how to respond to pressure, conflict, failure, success, and money. What you do often speaks so loudly your children can't hear what you are saying. In other words, your actions speak louder than your words.

The Jewish people had different ways of dealing with people according to their age. In the Talmud it talks of the ages of a man. The following list is taken from *The Paradigm Papers* in the chapter entitled, "Childhood and Adolescence" by Jeff Reed.

- 5 years is for reading (Scripture)

- 10 years for Misnah (The Law)

- 13 years for Commandments (Bar Mitzvah, moral responsibility)

- 15 years for Gemara (Talmudic discussions, abstract reasoning)

- 18 years for Hupa (Wedding Canopy)

- 20 years for seeking a livelihood (Pursuing an occupation)

- 30 years for attaining full strength (Koah)

- 40 years for understanding

- 50 years for giving counsel

- 60 years for becoming an elder (Wisdom, old age)

- 70 years for white hair

- 80 years for Gevurah (new, special strength of old age)

- 90 years for being bent under the weights of the years

- 100 years for being as if almost dead and passed away from the world[2]

Am I saying that we should specifically follow these instructions given to us from the Talmud? Of course not, but the point of the matter is that the norm among evangelical families today is that there is no process or no guidelines for the way we train our children or even plan our lives. Often, there is neither rhyme nor reason for what we do. Let us remember another old saying: "The person who fails to plan, plans to fail."

JOSHUA'S FAREWELL ADDRESS

> *And Joshua gathered all the tribes of Israel to Shechem, and called for the elders of Israel, and for their heads, and for their judges, and for their officers; and they presented themselves before God (Joshua 24:1).*

Before departing the scene, Joshua called for all the leaders of Israel, including the heads of all the families. During this address, he rehearsed their history of redemption from Egypt and God's faithfulness to their nation. Knowing by the word of the Lord their pending apostasy, he told them these very somber and powerful words that should be the theme of every head of household.

> *Now therefore fear the Lord, and serve Him in sincerity and in truth: and put away the gods which your fathers served on the other side of the flood, and in Egypt; and serve ye the Lord. And if it seem evil unto you to serve the Lord, choose you this*

day whom ye will serve; whether the gods which your fathers served that were on the other side of the flood, or the gods of the Amorites, in whose land ye dwell: **but as for me and my house, we will serve the Lord** (Joshua 24:14-15).

Joshua couldn't control what the other heads of households and leaders would do. He couldn't control the destiny of the whole nation of Israel. But the one thing he could do was to declare without hesitation that he and his house would serve the Lord!

Ultimately, I am not responsible for what other people do; I am only responsible for what I do for my God, with my time, to my family, as part of His Body, and the responsibility I have before God as a steward of all of the above.

In this day and age, with the cultural decline and various temptations, such as television, Facebook, and other online chatting venues that are readily available within the home, the only way we can survive and thrive as Christians is to make this declaration and follow it up with family discipleship and determination! We can't afford to totter on a fence with double-mindedness. We cannot declare that we will "try to serve the Lord" or "attempt to maintain a godly atmosphere in our homes." Satan will eat us up for breakfast if we are tentative instead of tenacious!

AS FOR ME AND MY HOUSE, WE WILL SERVE THE LORD

We need to first of all boldly declare that *as for me and my house, we will serve the Lord.* However, success requires more than just declarations with our mouths. We are going to have to work hard in our marriages, with our children, and in our churches. Church and home need to be integrated as the households and tribes of Israel were integrated into one nation. We must realize that the primary responsibility of discipling the children of Christian families rests not with the church leadership and church programs, but with the parents.

As a pastor, I often tell our congregation that one hour a week in Sunday school cannot counter the hours of worldly views instilled in our children through school, friends, and the media. Parents need to take the lead in the training and discipling of their children so that the influence of the home and the church can more effectively protect our children from the influences of the ungodly, humanistic mindsets of the world system. By and large, church leaders aren't responsible for the backslidden condition of the teenagers of Christian parents! Many parents have tried to blame the church programs or lack of friends in the church, but the responsibility for discipleship rests squarely on the shoulders of the parents.

I remember a few years ago, a parent in our church called me up complaining that her daughter had fallen away from the Lord because she wasn't connecting properly with our youth group. In essence, she was blaming the church for her teenage daughter's condition and self-destructive choices. I had to gently correct this mother by telling her that we only have her daughter for two hours a week as a church while, as the parent, she has responsibility for her daughter for the other 166 hours in the week. I told her that it was the job of the mother and father to disciple their children, with the church coming alongside them as an aid. The church was never designed to be a replacement for Christian parents. As we continued to discuss her daughter's situation, we discovered this girl had a large amount of unsupervised time on her computer, cell phone, and television, as well as no organized prayer and Bible devotional time together as a family. This parent came to see that it was not the church, but the parent's neglect, that was the primary blame for her daughter's condition.

As the spiritual leader goes, so goes the church; as the head of household goes, so goes the family.

In our local church, I was troubled by the fact that young people had no signposts of faith along the way that would serve as significant markers to give them more stability and traction as they grow older. This is essentially a challenge in non-denominational evangelical churches. In the same way a karate studio keeps kids motivated by a sense of accomplishment when they go through the progress of white belt to black belt, the church needs to have a protocol in place to do this for its young people.

In the early 2000s, we began to have confirmation classes for those in the seventh and eighth grades. We made it a combination of learning sound doctrine and learning about life. At the end they graduate, receive a chastity ring, and make a vow of serving the Lord the rest of their lives. My youngest son, Justin, went through the process when he was 11 years old, and it kept him pure, even when he underwent great temptation in high school and college. A few years ago we also started having First Communion classes for second and third graders, where we teach children the basics of the faith, Scripture memorization, and the Apostles' Creed. That has also become a great success and given our local church a powerful intergenerational plan for establishing the next generation of believers in the faith.

THINK ON THIS

Everything in the Kingdom of God starts and ends with the heads of households and families. One of the most powerful passages dealing with the biblical mandate to train up our children and maintain a godly household is found in Deuteronomy 6:1-9.

Read Deuteronomy 6:1-9 and answer the following questions pertaining to the need for training our children and maintaining a godly household.

How many generations did God say needed to be taught His commandments? (See verses 1-3.)

_____

_____

What does it mean to "diligently teach God's commandments to our children"? (See verses 4-8.)

_____

_____

_____

_____

Read Joshua 24:14-15. What advice does Joshua give in this passage?

_____

_____

_____

_____

What declaration did he make about his own household?

_____

_____

Make that your declaration today by writing it down, dating it, and signing it.

What changes are you going to make in your lifestyle to begin to keep this promise you just made to God?

_____

_____

_____

_____

_____

_____

_____

_____

Perhaps you might want to begin keeping a journal of what you want to do to begin training up the next generation in the ways of God. Record each of these lifestyle changes and the results you see in your children, your family, and even your church family.

ENDNOTES

1. Letter from Thomas Jefferson to Peter Carr, August 19, 1785, located online at http://avalon.law.yale.edu/18th_century/let31.asp.

2. Jeff Reed, *The Paradigm Papers: Church-Based Christian Education: Creating a New Paradigm–Part I: Childhood and Adolescence* (Ames, IA: LearnCorp, 1997), 14, located online at http://bild.org/download/paradigmPapers/3_Childhood-Adolescence.pdf.

CHAPTER 9

IT TAKES TIME

GOD started out with one man, Adam, and that didn't work out so well. He restarted the redemption process with Noah and then again with Abraham, then revealed Himself to each of Abraham's children, Isaac and Jacob. He started a nation from them who were eventually disinherited, displaced, and judged time and again because of their unfaithfulness. This up-and-down cycle took place for more than 40 generations until the fullness of time came when the promised Messiah would come. The redemption of God's people is a multigenerational process that cannot be expedited because of the short-sightedness and temporal longings of people. It takes time!

THE BOOK OF RUTH

We desperately need to catch the biblical vision of thinking and strategizing generationally. If the Jews didn't think in terms of multiple generations, then it is likely King David would have never made it as a great leader; perhaps he would have never been born!

David was a direct descendant of the patriarch Judah. Judah was one of the leaders in the Bible with a less than perfect past. The Bible records the story in Genesis 38 that Judah was tricked by his daughter-in-law Tamar into having sex with her when she disguised herself and he thought she was a prostitute. She did this because Judah unfairly kept back his youngest son, Shelah, from her because Judah feared he would be smitten by the Lord as his two other sons, Er and Onan, had been when they married her. In truth, Onan had refused to raise up seed for his brother Er. God killed Onan because he wouldn't build generationally!

According to Deuteronomy 23:2, none of Judah's descendants would be eligible to enter the ministry or be part of the assembly of the Lord for ten generations: "*A bastard shall not enter into the congregation of the Lord; even to his tenth generation shall he not enter into the congregation of the Lord.*"

Christians with a one-generation mindset could never have the vision or the patience to wait out what amounted to about 400 years of biblically nurturing their families and preparing the way for the prophetic word spoken over Judah in Genesis 49 to be fulfilled! "*The scepter shall not depart from Judah, nor a lawgiver from between his feet, until Shiloh come; and unto him shall the gathering of the people be*" (Gen. 49:10).

The amazing thing is, King David of the tribe of Judah, was exactly the tenth person listed genealogically in the Book of Ruth!

> *So Boaz took Ruth, and she was his wife: and when he went in unto her, the Lord gave her conception, and she bare a son. And the women said unto Naomi, Blessed be the Lord, which hath not left thee this day without a kinsman, that his name may be famous in Israel. And he shall be unto thee a restorer of thy life, and a nourisher of thine old age: for thy daughter in law, which loveth thee, which is better to thee than seven sons, hath born him. And Naomi took the child, and laid it in her bosom, and became nurse unto it. And the women her neighbours gave it a name, saying, There is a son born to Naomi; and they called his name Obed: he is the father of Jesse, the father of David. Now these are the generations of Pharez:*

Pharez begat Hezron, and Hezron begat Ram, and Ram begat Amminadab, and Amminadab begat Nahshon, and Nahshon begat Salmon, and Salmon begat Boaz, and Boaz begat Obed, and Obed begat Jesse, and Jesse begat David (Ruth 4:13-22).

Note the first person mentioned in this genealogy is Pharez, who was the child born as the result of the union between Judah and Tamar. You can count David as the tenth mentioned in this genealogy.

- 1st generation—Pharez

- 2nd generation—Hezron

- 3rd generation—Ram

- 4th generation—Amminadab

- 5th generation—Nahshon

- 6th generation—Salmon

- 7th generation—Boaz

- 8th generation—Obed

- 9th generation—Jesse

- 10th generation—David

Of course, the greatest example of this in the Bible is the many generations it took for God to prepare the way for the Messiah, Jesus Christ.

The book of the genealogy of Jesus Christ, the Son of David, the Son of Abraham:

Abraham begot Isaac, Isaac begot Jacob, and Jacob begot Judah and his brothers. Judah begot Perez and Zerah by Tamar, Perez begot Hezron, and Hezron begot Ram. Ram

begot Amminadab, Amminadab begot Nahshon, and Nah-
shon begot Salmon. Salmon begot Boaz by Rahab, Boaz begot
Obed by Ruth, Obed begot Jesse, and Jesse begot David the
king. David the king begot Solomon by her who had been
the wife of Uriah. Solomon begot Rehoboam, Rehoboam
begot Abijah, and Abijah begot Asa. Asa begot Jehoshaphat,
Jehoshaphat begot Joram, and Joram begot Uzziah. Uzziah
begot Jotham, Jotham begot Ahaz, and Ahaz begot Hezekiah.
Hezekiah begot Manasseh, Manasseh begot Amon, and Amon
begot Josiah. Josiah begot Jeconiah and his brothers about the
time they were carried away to Babylon. And after they were
brought to Babylon, Jeconiah begot Shealtiel, and Shealtiel
begot Zerubbabel. Zerubbabel begot Abiud, Abiud begot Elia-
kim, and Eliakim begot Azor. Azor begot Zadok, Zadok begot
Achim, and Achim begot Eliud. Eliud begot Eleazar, Eleazar
begot Matthan, and Matthan begot Jacob. And Jacob begot
Joseph the husband of Mary, of whom was born Jesus who is
called Christ. So all the generations from Abraham to David
are fourteen generations, from David until the captivity in
Babylon are fourteen generations, and from the captivity in
Babylon until the Christ are fourteen generations (Matthew
1:1-17 NKJV).

As you can see, it took 42 generations of preparation from Abraham
for the "Son of Abraham" to come forth! That's not including all the time
from Adam to Abraham and all those names not mentioned in the genealogies that would make it far more than the 42 generations mentioned
in Matthew! The genealogies in Scripture only mention the key names
of people necessary to trace the godly seed; the genealogical records in
Scripture are accurate, but not comprehensive.

THE POTENTIAL FOR DOMINION

To expound on the potential for dominion through the populating of the earth with covenantal children, I have included the following quotes from the book, *Prosperous Christians in an Age of Guilt Manipulators* by David Chilton.

> Their experience in Egypt testified to the astounding possibilities for population growth. If 3,000 covenanted household servants entered the land of Egypt with the 70 lineal descendants, then they multiplied to 2.5 million in about 135 years. How do we know this? Because the execution of the Hebrew males began about 80 years before the Exodus, and the total time that they spent in Egypt was about 215 years. This was understood by the writers of the Septuagint—the Greek language translation of the Old Testament—two centuries before the birth of Christ. They added to Exodus 12:40 the bracketed words. "Now the time that the sons of Israel lived in Egypt [and in the land of Canaan] was four hundred and thirty years." Paul informs us in Galatians 3:15-17 that it was 430 years from the Abrahamic covenant to the Exodus. So about half of this time was spent in Egypt.
>
> Thus, the growth from 3,000 (Or 10,000) to 2.5 million took place in the first two generations in Egypt. This points to large numbers of conversions to Judaism, and the adoption of these circumcised converts into the original twelve families. If 3,000 came to Egypt, then the growth rate was over 5% per annum—historically unprecedented in terms of births alone. If 10,000 came in, then the rate was about 4.17% per anuum—slightly higher than the extremely high 4.14% annual rate of increase of the incomparably fertile Hutterite communities in the

United States in the early 1950s. It is more likely that conversions accounted for much of this increase in Egypt. But the combination of births and conversions expanded the Hebrew population rapidly, as Pharaoh noted.

Had a rate of 4.17% per annum continued (let alone increased as a result of zero miscarriages), they would have multiplied from 2.5 million to 10 billion—almost twice today's total world population—in 197 years after the Exodus. This gives you some idea of the potential for growth which God's promise, coupled with a comparable rate of growth and conversions, offers. It means that within a century, the whole world of their day would have come to the true faith. But to have achieved this, they would have had to remain covenantally faithful. They didn't remain faithful.

The Dominion covenant is an ethical covenant. When men conform themselves rigorously to God's law, through God's grace they are to expect incomparable blessings. The whole earth is to come under covenant man's jurisdiction as rapidly as possible. The rule of God's law on earth is not to be delayed for "old time's sake." God offered the Hebrews world dominion when they entered Canaan. Canaan was little more than a point of embarkation.[1]

CURRENT DAY STRATEGIES

With the emphasis on escapist theology and the end times, is the current evangelical church willing to build generationally for success? I have said this earlier, but let me repeat it for emphasis: *If the evangelical church did nothing else but have the amount of biological children God wanted them to*

*have, disciple and keep those children in the faith, and prepare them to take the
lead in our nation, we would take back this country in one to two generations!*

The ironic thing is the current evangelical church in America is
being defeated in the cultural war by none other than the homosexual/
humanistic agenda. This consummate one-generational mindset is out-
thinking, out-maneuvering, and out-strategizing the one group of people
in the whole world that should defeat them by sheer numbers! The homosexuals have an average life span of about 45 years and have a culture of
generational death because they have no way to reproduce biologically as
partners after their own kind. They depend on reproducing their way of
thinking ideologically through the media and in the halls of higher learning; otherwise, they would just die out!

Our biggest challenge in terms of political and religious freedom in
America is the homosexual lobby, yet they should be the easiest group to
defeat because they are not self-perpetuating. Yet the evangelical church
has not done an effectual job of reaching out to those dealing with homosexuality. For the most part, the Church shuns these people and treats
them like pariahs, offering them no help with their internal struggles.
The Church needs to reach out and embrace them and enter into dialogue with leaders in their community.

Several years ago, one of the New York leaders of a gay advocacy
group, Soul Force, called and asked if they could attend services in our
church. When I consented, many of the church leaders were upset because
this organization attempts to infiltrate key evangelical churches for the
purpose of getting them to be open to and eventually accept homosexuality as a normal lifestyle. I told them that God was going to move and
that we had nothing to fear! The Sunday they came was very profound. I
preached a message regarding emotional health that comes only in Christ.
The leader and those who came with him from the Soul Force group were
weeping all the while I was ministering.

One of the young men came up to me after the service and thanked
me for teaching him the truth. He came forward during the altar call to

receive prayer for God's will to be done in his life. He even kept attend-ing our church for weeks afterward! Following the service, some of my leaders met with this Soul Force contingent and heard how impacted they were by the service. This group told my leaders they had never ever experienced the love of God in an evangelical church. Instead of fearing or shunning them, we need to embrace them and have dialogue with their leaders, as well as offer ministry to those who want to surrender their lives to Christ.

THINK ON THIS

The redemption of God's people is a multigenerational pro-cess that cannot be _____ because of the short-sightedness and temporal longings of people. It takes _____!

God killed Onan because he wouldn't build _____!

Even while slaves in Egypt, the Israelites could have reached the whole world of their day in one generation had they remained covenantally faithful to God. Did they reach the whole world?

_____

Why or why not?

_____

_____

When people conform themselves rigorously to God's law, they are to expect _____. After the Exodus from Egypt, God offered the Hebrews _____ when they entered Canaan.

The current evangelical Church in America is being defeated in the cultural war by _____.

ENDNOTE

1. David Chilton, *Productive Christians in an Age of Guilt Manipulators* (Tyler, TX: Institute for Christian Economics, 1985), 159-160.

CHAPTER 10

DISCIPLESHIP, IMPARTATION, REPRODUCTION, AND MULTIPLICATION

Our thoughts beget actions, which beget habits, which beget patterns of life, which beget our life's destination, which in turn passes on blessings or cursings to our children's children.
—Joseph Mattera

TOO often in the evangelical church, we think of blessings and curses as mere mantras and words spoken over people. Many saints spend a lot of time trying to discern curses spoken over them by witches and warlocks. While I am not belittling the importance of this, I will say that the biblical emphasis in regard to blessings and curses has more to do with obedience and disobedience than anything else.

When we read about putting on the whole armor of God in Ephesians 6:10-17, it is not referring to some mystical practice of putting pieces of powerful weaponry on us while in prayer. It is the summary passage of the first five and a half chapters. The first two chapters deal with knowing who we are in Christ. Chapters 3–6 instruct us how to live as the Body of Christ in the world.

Ephesians 4:27 warns us, *"neither give place to the devil."* How do we give place to the devil? To answer this, we have to read the entire passage surrounding this warning. Ephesians 4:25-32:

Verse 25 tells us we are not to lie to one another, *"Wherefore putting away lying, speak every man truth with his neighbor: for we are members one of another."*

Verse 26 tells us not to allow anger to fester inside of us, *"Be ye angry, and sin not: let not the sun go down upon your wrath."*

Verse 28 continues our instructions by warning us not to steal or refuse to work for a living, *"Let him that stole steal no more: but rather let him labour, working with his hands the thing which is good, that he may have to give to him that needed."*

Verse 29 cautions us to watch what comes out of our mouths, *"Let no corrupt communication proceed out of your mouth, but that which is good to the use of edifying, that it may minister grace unto the hearers."*

If we allow bitterness, wrath, clamor, and unforgiveness to rule our lives, and if we refuse to treat one another with kindness and forgiveness, we are not putting on the armor of God—we are giving the devil a foothold (see Eph. 4:30-32). When we live a lifestyle that creates negative habits and an ungodly atmosphere in our homes, it gives our children the pattern for their lives. When they have their own families, this cycle is then repeated in their children. This is what is referred to in Exodus 20:5-6:

> *...I the Lord thy God am a jealous God, visiting the iniquity of the fathers upon the children unto the third and fourth generation of them that hate Me; And showing mercy unto thousands of them that love Me, and keep My commandments.*

The main idea here is that God will appoint or allow the same kind of behavior the parents are involved in to be passed down to their children because of the generational connection that is legally binding on them.

The emphasis is on obeying God's commandments to receive blessing instead of perpetuating disobedience in future generations.[1]

Parents determine whether there is a blessing or curse on their children and on their home. Please take time to read and pray over Psalm 78:1-8, where this powerful principle is repeated for us again:

> Give ear, O my people, to my law: incline your ears to the words of My mouth. I will open my mouth in a parable: I will utter dark sayings of old: which we have heard and known, and our fathers have told us. We will not hide them from their children, showing to the generation to come the praises of the Lord, and His strength, and His wonderful works that He hath done. For He established a testimony in Jacob, and appointed a law in Israel, which He commanded our fathers, that they should make them known to their children: that the generation to come might know them, even the children which should be born; who should arise and declare them to their children: That they might set their hope in God, and not forget the works of God, but keep His commandments: And might not be as their fathers, a stubborn and rebellious generation; a generation that set not their heart aright, and whose spirit was not stedfast with God.

If we would spend more time meditating on the law of God and allow the grace of God to walk it out in full view of our children, we would perpetuate the greatest generational blessing that this nation has yet to see.

THE LIFE OF DAVID

The greatest example of the aforementioned principles of blessing and cursing can be found in the life of David, as recorded in First Samuel and Second Samuel. We will see that the lifestyle we choose not only positively affects our biological children, but those under our particular sphere of influence as well.

DAVID'S POSITIVE INFLUENCE: 1 SAMUEL 22:1-3

David had a positive influence on those who were in debt, distress, and discontented as they lived with him, submitted to him, and observed him in warfare. They became an army that kept growing in numbers and eventually became known as David's Mighty Men (see 2 Sam. 23:8-39; 1 Chron. 12). God had prepared David, and then David reproduced himself in these previously unprofitable men!

David killed a lion in First Samuel 17:34-36. Benaiah killed a lion in Second Samuel 23:20. David killed a giant in First Samuel 17:50. Three of his men killed giants in First Chronicles 20:4-8. David submitted to authority and was loyal to God's chosen king in First Samuel 18:5. In turn, his men submitted to his authority and were loyal to him in First Chronicles 12:33,38. David worshiped God in spirit and was a prophet and psalmist who wrote 75 of the psalms in the Old Testament (see 1 Sam. 16:23; 1 Chron. 16:7). Through his example, 288 of his men worshiped in spirit and sang the songs of the Lord, as recorded in First Chronicles 16:4-6 and 25:1-7.

DAVID'S NEGATIVE INFLUENCE: 2 SAMUEL 11:1-12:7

Although David was a great warrior and worshiper, it seems as though he was not a good father to his children. Unfortunately the laws of impartation and reproduction worked negatively to the detriment of his family. Children are either trained in the way they should go or in the way they should not go by our example.

David was guilty of the sins of idleness, pride, lust, lying, murder, and adultery, as recorded in Second Samuel 11:1-12:7. His sins with a woman were reproduced in his natural sons. Amnon's sin with a woman is recorded in Second Samuel 13:1-19. Absolam's sin of murder because of a woman, just like his father David, is recorded in Second Samuel 13:20-33. Absolam's ultimate way of shaming his father David was by lying with David's concubines in Second Samuel 16:20-22. Adonijah's untimely death was sealed because of desiring a woman in First Kings 2:13-25. Even wise King Solomon's downfall and apostasy was caused by desiring women (see 1 Kings 11:1-8). Sin is multiplied generationally. David fell with one woman; Solomon officially had 1,000—that we know of!

Was it a coincidence that all of David's sons' failures had something to do with a woman, or was it because of the laws of impartation resulting in reproduction and multiplication of the same behavior? The curse brought upon his sons had everything to do with David's adultery and murder and had nothing to do with witchcraft, incantations, and demonic objects in his house. David was a great psalmist and soldier, but seemed to be a miserable family man and natural father!

STATISTICAL PROOF

Leonard Ravenhill demonstrates the principles espoused in this chapter when he contrasts the life of atheist Max Jukes with that of the godly evangelist Jonathon Edwards in his masterful book, *Sodom Had No Bible*.[2]

Atheist Max Jukes

Lived an ungodly life. He married an ungodly girl and from this union:

310 died as paupers

150 were criminals

7 were murderers

100 were drunkards

More than half the women were prostitutes

His 540 descendants cost the state more than one and a quarter million dollars!

Evangelist Jonathon Edwards

Lived the same time as Jukes but married a godly girl. Of his 1,394 descendants:

100 preachers and missionaries

13 became college presidents

65 college professors

3 United States Senators

30 Judges

100 lawyers

60 physicians

75 army and navy officers

60 authors of prominence

1 V.P. of the United States

80 public officials in other capacities

295 college graduates

Some were governors of states

His descendants cost the state nothing!

THINK ON THIS

Take a moment to consider what kind of influence you are having on your family.

Are your biological and spiritual children learning positive or negative life patterns from your example in the home?

_____

Ask yourself the following questions concerning the life patterns you and your spouse learned from your parents and compare them with those you are now passing on to your own children. I suggest each spouse answer the questions independently and then come together and discuss your answers.

How did my parents handle conflict?

How do I handle conflict with my spouse?

How did my parents manage their money?

How do I manage my family finances?

How did my parents show affection toward one another?

How do I show affection to my spouse?

How did my parents communicate with one another?

How do I communicate with my spouse?

How did my parents relate to their children? How am I relating to my children?

What was my parents' work ethic?

What is my work ethic?

How did my parents relate to their parents?

How am I relating to my parents?

How well did my parents submit to authority figures?

How well do I submit to those in authority over my life?

How did my parents process emotional and/or physical pain?

How do I process pain?

How well did my parents emotionally connect with others?

How well do I emotionally connect to others?

Did my parents enjoy intimate, authentic relationships with others?

Do I enjoy intimate, authentic relationships with others?

What were my parents' eating habits?

What are my eating habits?

What were my parents' habits in regard to exercise?

What are my patterns in regard to exercise?

ENDNOTES

1. The key word to understand in the passage of Exodus is the phrase "visiting the iniquity." The Hebrew word for *visit* is: [*paqad* /paw·kad/ to attend to, muster, number, reckon, visit, punish, appoint, look after, care for. 1a (*Qal*). 1a1 to pay attention to, observe. 1a2 to attend to. 1a3 to seek, look about for. 1a4 to seek in vain, need, miss, lack. 1a5 to visit. 1a6 to visit upon, punish. 1a7 to pass in review, muster, number. 1a8 to appoint, assign, lay upon as a charge, deposit. 1b (*Niphal*). 1b1 to be sought, be needed, be missed, be lacking. 1b2 to be visited. 1b3 to be visited upon. 1b4 to be appointed. 1b5 to be watched over. 1c (*Piel*) to muster, call up. 1d (*Pual*) to be passed in review, be caused to miss, be called, be called to account. 1e (*Hiphil*). 1e1 to set over, make overseer, appoint an overseer. 1e2 to commit, entrust, commit for care, deposit. 1f (*Hophal*). 1f1 to be visited. 1f2 to be deposited. 1f3 to be made overseer, be entrusted. 1g (*Hithpael*) numbered. 1h (*Hothpael*) numbered. 2 musterings, expenses.] *Brown-Driver-Briggs Hebrew Lexicon*, s.v. "paqad," H6485.

2. Leonard Ravenhill, *Sodom Had No Bible* (Pensacola, FL: Christian Life Books, 2007), 155.

CHAPTER 11

GOD REMEMBERS

The memory of the just is blessed (Proverbs 10:7).

MOST folks get bored when they read the genealogies mentioned in Scripture. So and so begot so and so who begot...and so forth. However, when you begin to understand the importance of generations and how powerfully they affect the way we are today, it motivates you to know your history. You can't fully know who you are in terms of your human experience unless you know where you came from.

THE SINS OF OUR FATHERS

Does God deal with us according to our history? Although there are many who believe that God doesn't hold us responsible for the sins of our fathers, the Bible teaches us that we become the recipients of both bless-ing and curses according to our generational connection. Read Second Samuel 21:1-3:

> Now there was a famine in the days of David for three years, year after year; and David inquired of the Lord. And the Lord answered, "It is because of Saul and his bloodthirsty house, because he killed the Gibeonites." So the king called the Gibeonites and spoke to them. Now the Gibeonites were not

of the children of Israel, but of the remnant of the Amorites; the children of Israel had sworn protection to them, but Saul had sought to kill them in his zeal for the children of Israel and Judah. Therefore David said to the Gibeonites, "What shall I do for you? And with what shall I make atonement, that you may bless the inheritance of the Lord?" (2 Samuel 21:1-3 NKJV)

In this story we see King David and the nation of Israel, who represented the second generation of leadership from King Saul, being judged with a three-year famine because of the bloodletting of King Saul in the previous generation. Not only that, but David had to allow the Gibeonites to slaughter seven of the sons of King Saul in order to rectify this inequity, even though said sons were not personally involved in the egregious actions of their father!

And the Gibeonites said unto him, We will have no silver nor gold of Saul, nor of his house; neither for us shalt thou kill any man in Israel. And he said, What ye shall say, that will I do for you. And they answered the king, The man that consumed us, and that devised against us that we should be destroyed from remaining in any of the coasts of Israel, let seven men of his sons be delivered unto us, and we will hang them up unto the Lord in Gibeah of Saul, whom the Lord did choose. And the king said, I will give them. But the king spared Mephibosheth, the son of Jonathan the son of Saul, because of the Lord's oath that was between them, between David and Jonathan the son of Saul. But the king took the two sons of Rizpah the daughter of Aiah, whom she bare unto Saul, Armoni and Mephibosheth; and the five sons of Michal the daughter of Saul, whom she brought up for Adriel the son of Barzillai the Meholathite: And he delivered them into the hands of the Gibeonites, and they hanged them in the hill before the Lord: and they fell all seven together, and were put to death in the days of harvest, in the first days, in the beginning of barley harvest (2 Samuel 21:4-9).

This passage of Scripture clearly communicates—**God remembers!**

THE GENEALOGY OF JESUS

We can get a glimpse into who Jesus is by examining the lives of those God picked to represent His genealogy.

The book of the genealogy of Jesus Christ, the Son of David, the Son of Abraham: **Abraham** *begot* **Isaac**, *Isaac begot* **Jacob**, *and Jacob begot Judah and his brothers. Judah begot Perez and Zerah by Tamar, Perez begot Hezron, and Hezron begot Ram. Ram begot Amminadab, Amminadab begot Nahshon, and Nahshon begot Salmon. Salmon begot Boaz by* **Rahab**, *Boaz begot Obed by* **Ruth**, *Obed begot Jesse, and Jesse begot* **David the king.** *David the king begot* **Solomon** *by her who had been the wife of Uriah. Solomon begot Rehoboam, Rehoboam begot Abijah, and Abijah begot Asa. Asa begot Jehoshaphat, Jehoshaphat begot Joram, and Joram begot Uzziah. Uzziah begot Jotham, Jotham begot Ahaz, and Ahaz begot Hezekiah. Hezekiah begot Manasseh, Manasseh begot Amon, and Amon begot Josiah. Josiah begot Jeconiah and his brothers about the time they were carried away to Babylon. And after they were brought to Babylon, Jeconiah begot Shealtiel, and Shealtiel begot Zerubbabel. Zerubbabel begot Abiud, Abiud begot Eliakim, and Eliakim begot Azor. Azor begot Zadok, Zadok begot Achim, and Achim begot Eliud. Eliud begot Eleazar, Eleazar begot Matthan, and Matthan begot Jacob. And Jacob begot Joseph the husband of Mary, of whom was born Jesus who is called Christ. So all the* *generations from Abraham to David are fourteen generations, from David until the captivity in Babylon are fourteen genera- tions, and from the captivity in Babylon until the Christ are fourteen generations* (Matthew 1:1-17).

When examining this genealogy, we see how some of the names speak powerfully to the background and makeup of the Lord Jesus. The King of kings descended from great men and women of God, but also from sinners with a sordid past. This speaks to us about how He identified Himself with humanity to such an extent that even His past is numbered with the sin- ners, though He Himself was without sin (see 2 Cor. 5:21).

Abraham was the father of the faithful and the progenitor of the godly seed that produced Christ in the natural and the Church in the Spirit. *Isaac* became the child of promise who represents the fulfillment of vision and who was a type of Jesus when he was almost offered up to God in sacrifice on Mount Moriah (see Gen. 22). *Jacob* represents a person whose pride was broken by the trials of life and who lived to see 70 of his descen- dents and the beginning of the nation of Israel. *Judah* represented not only the tribe that Jesus descended from, but also sinful humanity because he slept with his daughter-in-law thinking she was a prostitute (see Gen. 38). *Rahab* the prostitute and Gentile is also in Jesus' history and geneal- ogy (see Josh. 2). *Ruth* the Moabite was another Gentile, but also a great woman of destiny!

DAVID: THE GREATEST KING OF ISRAEL

David was a combination king, prophet, priest, psalmist, and war- rior—all of which speak to different aspects of the earthly ministry of the Lord Jesus Christ. Most importantly, David is the king God chose to per- petuate His eternal Kingdom by bringing forth the Christ. King David, in spite of his sins and shortcomings, was the greatest leader Israel ever had.

The favor of God was upon him. Even the New Testament testifies that David was a man who fulfilled God's purpose for his generation.

> *...they desired a king: and God gave unto them Saul the son of Cis, a man of the tribe of Benjamin, by the space of forty years. And when he had removed him, he raised up unto them David to be their king; to whom also he gave their testimony, and said, I have found David the son of Jesse, a man after mine own heart, which shall fulfil all my will. Of this man's seed hath God according to his promise raised unto Israel a Saviour, Jesus (Acts 13:21-23).*

> *Wherefore he saith also in another psalm, Thou shalt not suffer Thine Holy One to see corruption. For David, after he had served his own generation by the will of God, fell on sleep, and was laid unto his fathers, and saw corruption (Acts 13:35-36).*

Because of the principle of generational blessing, all the descendants of David who succeeded Him on the throne were able to cash in on the "divine capital" he had accrued.

> *And when thy days be fulfilled, and thou shalt sleep with thy fathers, I will set up thy seed after thee, which shall proceed out of thy bowels, and I will establish his kingdom. He shall build an house for My name, and I will stablish the throne of his kingdom for ever. I will be his father, and he shall be My son. If he commit iniquity, I will chasten him with the rod of men, and with the stripes of the children of men: But My mercy shall not depart away from him, as I took it from Saul, whom I put away before thee. And thine house and thy kingdom shall be established for ever before thee: thy throne shall be established for ever (2 Samuel 7:12-16).*

This pattern of blessing people because of the obedience and covenant God made with their ancestor began all the way in the Book of Genesis with Abraham, Isaac, and Jacob.

God spoke to Isaac in Genesis 26:3-5:

> Sojourn in this land, and I will be with thee, and will bless thee; for unto thee, and unto thy seed, I will give all these countries, and **I will perform the oath which I sware unto Abraham thy father**; and I will make thy seed to multiply as the stars of heaven, and will give unto thy seed all these countries; and in thy seed shall all the nations of the earth be blessed; because that Abraham obeyed My voice, and kept My charge, My commandments, My statutes, and My laws.

God made a covenant with David that his kingdom and throne would be established forever. This covenant became the basis for the "borrowed capital" his descendants lived off of for the blessings they as kings received. Solomon did not suffer the full consequences for his immorality because God remembered His covenant with David.

> And the Lord was angry with Solomon, because his heart was turned from the Lord God of Israel, which had appeared unto him twice, and had commanded him concerning this thing, that he should not go after other gods: but he kept not that which the Lord commanded. Wherefore the Lord said unto Solomon, Forasmuch as this is done of thee, and thou hast not kept My covenant and My statutes, which I have commanded thee, I will surely rend the kingdom from thee, and will give it to thy servant. Notwithstanding in thy days I will not do it for David thy father's sake: but I will rend it out of the hand of thy son. **Howbeit I will not rend away all the kingdom; but will give one tribe to thy son for David My servant's sake,**

and for Jerusalem's sake which I have chosen (1 Kings 11:9-13).

First Kings 11:36 says, "*And unto his son will I give one tribe, that David My servant may have a light alway before Me in Jerusalem.*"

God always referred back to David when dealing with the kings. See what is meant here.

God told *Jeroboam* that he didn't measure up to David in First Kings 14:7-9:

> *Go, tell Jeroboam, Thus saith the Lord God of Israel, For-asmuch as I exalted thee from among the people, and made thee prince over My people Israel, And rent the kingdom away from the house of David, and gave it thee: and* **yet thou hast not been as My servant David, who kept My commandments, and who followed Me with all his heart, to do that only which was right in Mine eyes**; *but hast done evil above all that were before thee....*

God also compared *Abijam* with his father David in First Kings 15:1-5:

> *Now in the eighteenth year of king Jeroboam the son of Nebat reigned Abijam over Judah. Three years reigned he in Jerusalem. And his mother's name was Maachah, the daughter of Abishalom. And he walked in all the sins of his father, which he had done before him:* **and his heart was not perfect with the Lord his God, as the heart of David his father. Nevertheless for David's sake did the Lord his God give him a lamp in Jerusalem, to set up his son after him, and to establish Jerusalem**: *Because David did that which was right in the eyes of the Lord, and turned not aside from any thing that He commanded him all the days of his life, save only in the matter of Uriah the Hittite.*

David's son *Asa* was more favorably compared to his father in First Kings 15:9-12:

> And in the twentieth year of Jeroboam king of Israel reigned Asa over Judah. And forty and one years reigned he in Jerusalem. And his mother's name was Maachah, the daughter of Abishalom. **And Asa did that which was right in the eyes of the Lord, as did David his father**. And he took away the sodomites out of the land, and removed all the idols that his fathers had made.

Though *Jehoram* did evil in the sight of the Lord, God did not destroy Judah because of His promise to David.

> And in the fifth year of Joram the son of Ahab king of Israel, Jehoshaphat being then king of Judah, Jehoram the son of Jehoshaphat king of Judah began to reign. Thirty and two years old was he when he began to reign; and he reigned eight years in Jerusalem. And he walked in the way of the kings of Israel, as did the house of Ahab: for the daughter of Ahab was his wife: and he did evil in the sight of the Lord. **Yet the Lord would not destroy Judah for David His servant's sake, as He promised him to give him alway a light , and to his children** (2 Kings 8:16-19).

Though *Amaziah* did that which was right in the sight of the Lord, he could not compare to his father David.

> In the second year of Joash son of Jehoahaz king of Israel reigned Amaziah the son of Joash king of Judah. He was twenty and five years old when he began to reign, and reigned twenty and nine years in Jerusalem. And his mother's name was Jehoaddan of Jerusalem. **And he did that which was right in the**

sight of the Lord, yet not like David his father: he did *according to all things as Joash his father did* (2 Kings 14:1-3).

In Second Kings 16:1-3, we read that Ahaz:

reigned sixteen years in Jerusalem, and did not do that which was right in the sight of the Lord his God, like David his father. But he walked in the way of the kings of Israel.

In Second Kings 18:1-3 it says:

Now it came to pass in the third year of Hoshea son of Elah king of Israel, that **Hezekiah** *the son of Ahaz king of Judah began to reign. Twenty and five years old was he when he began to reign; and he reigned twenty and nine years in Jerusalem. His mother's name also was Abi, the daughter of Zachariah. And* **he did that which was right in the sight of the Lord, according to all that David his father did.**

God identified Himself to *Hezekiah* as *the God of David* when He sent Isaiah to prophesy healing to him. It seems as though even the blessing of divine healing and health was connected to the memory of David.

In those days was **Hezekiah** *sick unto death. And the prophet Isaiah the son of Amoz came to him, and said unto him, Thus saith the Lord, Set thine house in order; for thou shalt die, and not live. Then he turned his face to the wall, and prayed unto the Lord, saying, I beseech thee, O Lord, remember now how I have walked before Thee in truth and with a perfect heart, and have done that which is good in Thy sight. And Hezekiah wept sore. And it came to pass, afore Isaiah was gone out into the middle court, that the word of the Lord came to him, saying, Turn again, and tell* **Hezekiah** *the captain of My people,* **Thus saith the Lord, the God of David thy father, I have heard thy prayer,** *I have seen thy tears: behold, I will heal thee: on the* *third day thou shalt go up unto the house of the Lord* (2 Kings 20:1-5).

Here are two more instances in which David's righteous descendents were identified with him:

> **Josiah** *was eight years old when he began to reign, and he reigned thirty and one years in Jerusalem. And his mother's name was Jedidah, the daughter of Adaiah of Boscath.* **And he did that which was right in the sight of the Lord, and walked in all the way of David his father**, *and turned not aside to the right hand or to the left* (2 Kings 22:1-2).

> And **Jehoshaphat** *his son reigned in his stead, and strengthened himself against Israel. And he placed forces in all the fenced cities of Judah, and set garrisons in the land of Judah, and in the cities of Ephraim, which Asa his father had taken.* And **the Lord was with Jehoshaphat, because he walked in the first ways of his father David**, *and sought not unto Baalim* (2 Chronicles 17:1-3).

HONOR THY FATHER AND MOTHER

As we can see in the history of the kings of Israel and Judah, God does remember. We can be the recipients of the generational blessing of our godly parents, both spiritual and biological. We also see the importance of obeying the fifth commandment as the apostle Paul reiterated in Ephesians 6:2-3:

> *Children, obey your parents in the Lord: for this is right. Honour thy father and mother; which is the first commandment*

with promise; **That it may be well with thee, and thou mayest live long on the earth** (Ephesians 6:2-3).

Those who think this is just an Old Testament principle must realize that Paul the apostle is quoting the fifth commandment from the Book of Exodus and declaring to Christians everywhere that they will receive blessings and long life by honoring their fathers and mothers! Hebrew thought and tradition was that the fifth commandment applied to honoring their spiritual fathers and the patriarchs in their history as well as their natural parents.

In this humanistic culture based on youth, it seems we honor and glorify only sex, power, and money. When I was growing up, kids on buses or subways would give up their seat for a woman or an older person. Now, I see pregnant women and old people with packages standing and not one young person has enough respect to offer them a seat. We can learn how much a person really knows about generational blessings by how they treat the older people around them.

In the West we are afraid to get old because we don't honor and respect age, history, or the past. We need to understand that according to the Bible, the grey head is an honor because of the wisdom that accompanies the years of experience it represents (see Prov. 20:29). I would much rather spend one hour with an old, seasoned warrior of God and glean from that person than hang out all day with a celebrity who hasn't proven, through many years, to be faithful and fruitful in ministry.

To some extent, the Church has been brainwashed by the youth-oriented culture and has adopted a superstar mentality just like the world! Many times we honor the best looking, best dressed, biggest ministry in town because it appeals to our need for success. I am not against having large or successful ministries, as long as they measure up to the standards of the Word of God. What I am against is coddling up to some of these "flash in the pan ministers" who never do anything to build the Church, but are only interested in blowing in, blowing out, and taking with them the money and resources that the communities they visit need!

When I am with young ministers, all they want to know about is my ministry. When I am with seasoned ministers with years behind them, the first thing they want to know is how I am doing with my family. One of the biggest problems we have in the Church today is that many young ministers don't have spiritual parents whom they look up to and receive from. All pastors should have pastors they are accountable to. If you can't tell someone who your spiritual oversight is, even as a minister, you are an accident waiting to happen!

The Bible teaches us to rise in the presence of the aged (see Lev. 19:32). This is something we would do automatically if we really understood the contents of this chapter. There is a powerful story in First Kings 12 that teaches the importance older, godly people can have in our lives. After Rehoboam became king of Israel in the place of his father, Solomon, the first thing he did when confronted with a challenge to his throne was to go to the aged men who stood before his father and ask their advice. But Rehoboam rejected their counsel and foolishly listened to his young friends who contradicted the sage advice given by the aged men. The result was the kingdom was divided, and he was left with only one of the 12 tribes. How important is it that we obey God's command when it comes to generational blessing?

THINK ON THIS

The memory of the just is blessed... (Proverbs 10:7).

Does God deal with us according to our history? (Read Second Samuel 21:1-3.)

What does it say in Second Samuel 21:3-9 about God's memory?

_____

_____

When examining this genealogy, we see how some of the names speak powerfully to the background and makeup of the Lord Jesus. List the names of those in your genealogy; then record what you believe they passed on to your generation, whether good or bad.

_____

_____

_____

_____

_____

_____

_____

_____

_____

_____

CHAPTER 12

MY STORY, MY FAMILY

O ye seed of Israel His servant, ye children of Jacob, His chosen ones. He is the Lord our God; His judgments are in all the earth. Be ye mindful always of His covenant; the word which He commanded to a thousand generations; even of the covenant which He made with Abraham, and of His oath unto Isaac; and hath confirmed the same to Jacob for a law, and to Israel for an everlasting covenant (1 Chronicles 16:13-17).

MY whole Christian life I have been building upon the prayers and actions of my grandmother and mother who have both gone before me. I thank God that they passed their faith down to me! One reason I have been able to write this book is because of how grateful I am to those who have gone before me, both in the spirit and in the natural. Going back just three generations, I am a person with a multiethnic background, with two primary ethnicities being Puerto Rican and Italian. My mother was born in Puerto Rico, with traces of English, French, and Castilian in her ancestry. My dad was a second-generation Italian. My grandmother, Antoinette Calder, came to New York from Puerto Rico when my mother Miriam was only a toddler. Eventually, my mother moved to New York to be with her mother when she was 7 years old.

THANK GOD FOR A PRAYING GRANDMOTHER!

My grandmother divorced her husband because of adultery and other serious issues and was rejected by the Catholic church. One day, as she was walking down the street, heartbroken over being rejected by her church, she came across a little Pentecostal church that met in a storefront. She went inside and received Jesus as Lord. Up until that time, nobody in her family had known Jesus personally.

Being on fire for God, my grandmother prayed three hours a day and preached on her street corner daily. Within a few years, she started a storefront mission that she led for almost 60 years. I read in a newspaper article, which the family saved for over 60 years, that said she was the "first ordained Hispanic minister in New York City history!" Thousands walked into that mission, came to Christ, and became ministers of the Gospel. My mother told me that there were always homeless people sleeping in the mission and in their house. It was a lifestyle of total surrender for Christ and the multitudes He loved and died for that she passed on to her future generations. But perhaps the most powerful aspect of her life was that by the time she died in her 80s, she had faithfully prayed almost her whole family into the Kingdom of God!

I know that is no coincidence, because on my father's side of the family, there had not been one person I know of who is serving the Lord except my dad. However, on my mother's side of the family, I have heard of cousins and relatives in Puerto Rico, California, New Jersey, and parts of New York who are serving the Lord and are in the ministry. My mother's nephew is a deacon in a church, two of his daughters are married to pastors, and a cousin in California pastors a church with over 1,000 in attendance!

My mother's brother would hold Bible studies. These are only the family members I know about. I am sure there are many more in the ministry whom I will meet in Heaven. Hallelujah!

Can you imagine the exponential blessing that will take place if all the Christian descendants of my grandmother continue to faithfully serve the Lord? What she experienced in her life in regard to seeing most of her family saved would be repeated, and each one of her offspring would then perpetuate the generational blessing with their own offspring!

Although my grandmother's children didn't always serve God in their youth, both my mother and her two siblings eventually began to serve the Lord when they were in their 40s and 50s. The faithful prayers all those years are what brought my mom, me, and much of our family to Christ. For this I will always be grateful to the memory of my grandmother and, of course, my mom, who took me to church when I was a teenager and was the primary person responsible for bringing me to faith in Christ.

MY STORY

I converted to Christianity when I was 19. By the time I was 21, I was ready to marry. Before we got married, Joyce and I fasted and prayed for three days for God to speak to us about whether or not it was God's will for us to be together. When we came back together, I told Joyce that God had given me a Scripture. She looked surprised because she said God had given her a Scripture as well. To our shock, God had given us both the same verses! Out of the 66 books in the Bible, what are the chances of that happening? The verse that He gave us was Malachi 2:15, which reads, *"And did not He make one? Yet had He the residue of the spirit. And wherefore one? That He might seek a godly seed...."*

God was showing us the main reason He was calling us to be married. We were to provide Him with godly seed. Being with the old evangelical mindset, for many years I thought that was only referring to winning souls and raising up spiritual children, but now I know that it refers to both spiritual and natural children.

We have been in full-time ministry officially since August 1980. We used our wedding money to go and preach in the old Soviet Union for six weeks. Since 1984, we have led the congregation we founded and have been blessed with many spiritual sons and daughters. We have also been blessed with five biological children. All of them have been raised in church and have been involved in various inner city ministries in New York City or in short-term mission work. Moreover, academically they are all excelling beyond what I ever imagined! We know that God is going to continue to use them mightily! Here is just a quick snapshot of what our five children have experienced and accomplished thus far.

(Note: I do not claim to have a perfect Christian family without the typical challenges. For example, during the writing of this book, one of my children has struggled greatly in the faith and has been the focus of much strategic-level intercession.)

My oldest son is the author of a *New York Times* bestseller (at age 26) and the editor of a major national newspaper. Our oldest daughter works for a hedge fund as an analyst. Our youngest son served as the president of a college campus ministry, and currently serves as the youth director of our church. One of our teenage daughters serves as a small group leader for the youth in our church and is on the youth preaching and worship team. Her preaching CDs have been favorites even among the adults in our church. Our youngest daughter has been serving in the youth ministry since the age of 12 and even teaches on occasion for the offering devotional and is also a small group leader.

Of course this doesn't include our many spiritual children. For example, we took one young man under our roof as our spiritual son who lived with us for years. All of my biological children consider him their full brother. He is now helping lead our congregation as a full-time minister and director of ministries. His natural father died when he was very young. After he came to Christ, I took him under my wing in the spirit and in the natural.

When my wife and I pray for our children, we are already praying for their children's children and blessing their family lines and their generations! God, who knows the future as well as the past, already sees them as the progenitors of godly seed as my wife and I intercede for them in accordance with that view.

Last but not least, my wife, Joyce, has been serving with me in full-time ministry since 1980 and pastoring with me since we founded Resurrection Church in 1980. She has her own business and founded Children of the City (COC), a community-based, tax-exempt corporation that has reached out to thousands of "at risk" youth in New York City since 1981.[1] COC currently has about 1,000 children on our active roster whose families are visited once a month by our 50 volunteers, most of whom attend our local church. Joyce was the worship leader of our church for many years and also works with many of the women and ministry leaders in our church. She has a profound teaching ministry and also a powerful ability in intercession and prophetic prayer.

Joyce and I are believing for great things, not only in our lifetime, but generationally. We are building the church and our family generationally because when we are long gone, we want to be like faithful Abel who, *"being dead yet speaketh"* (Heb. 11:4).

If your church or ministry reaches its highest level of impact during your lifetime, you have failed to fulfill your mission!

Jesus built generationally so that those who came after Him would outdo Him in terms of their ministerial works. John 14:12 states:

> *Verily, verily, I say unto you, He that believeth on Me, the works that I do shall he do also; and greater works than these shall he do; because I go unto My Father.*

God often identified Himself as the God of Abraham, Isaac, and Jacob. He has called every one of us to build our families and ministries to a minimum of three generations!

The covenant He made with His people was for a thousand generations! There haven't even been that many generations of people since the time of Adam; therefore, the blessing of First Chronicles 16:14-17 hasn't run out yet:

> *He is the Lord our God; His judgments are in all the earth. Be ye mindful always of His covenant; the word which He commanded to a thousand generations; even of the covenant which He made with Abraham, and of His oath unto Isaac; and hath confirmed the same to Jacob....*

THINK ON THIS

If your church or ministry reaches its highest level of impact during your lifetime, you have _____ _____ _____ _____ _____ _____!

List your biological children and your spiritual children. Start by asking God for a scriptural vision for each one. Then begin to pray that vision into their lives. Also remember to begin praying for godly spouses for them and for their children's children as well.

_____

_____

_____

ENDNOTE

1. Visit www.childrenofthecity.org for more information.

CHAPTER 13

IT'S A FAMILY AFFAIR

The Gospel is never meant just for individuals; the plan of God is for whole households to be carriers of the faith. — Joseph Mattera

THE FAMILY OF JOHN THE BAPTIST

MANY don't realize the powerful, godly families that were behind both the Lord Jesus and John the Baptist. Many think that John just appeared out of nowhere, but the Jews of that day knew the family of John. The spiritual lineage of John the Baptist was full of godly character and faithful service to the Lord.

> *There was in the days of Herod, the king of Judaea, **a certain priest named Zacharias, of the course of Abia: and his wife was of the daughters of Aaron, and her name was Elisabeth. And they were both righteous before God, walking in all the commandments and ordinances of the Lord blameless.** And they had no child, because that Elisabeth was barren, and they both were now well stricken in years. And it came to pass, that while he executed the priest's office before God in the order of his course, according to the*

> *custom of the priest's office, his lot was to burn incense when he went into the temple of the Lord. And the whole multitude of the people were praying without at the time of incense* (Luke 1:5-10).

Zacharias, the father of John the Baptist, was serving God faithfully in the ministry as a priest in the temple. We can trace Zacharias all the way back to Abiathar the priest, a descendant of Aaron.

Matthew Henry traces Abiathar back to Aaron for us.

> When in David's time the family of Aaron was multiplied, he divided them into twenty-four courses, for the more regular performances of their office, that it might never be either *neglected* for want of hands or *engrossed* by a few. The eighth of those was that of *Abia* (1 Chron. 24:10), who was descended from Eleazar, Aaron's eldest son.[1]

We can also trace Elizabeth to the priestly line of Aaron, as recorded in *Matthew Henry's Commentary,*

> The wife of this Zacharias was of the daughters of Aaron too, and her name was *Elisabeth*, the very same name with *Elisheba* the wife of Aaron, Exod. 6:23. The priest (Josephus saith) was very careful to marry within their own family, that they might maintain the dignity of the priesthood and keep it without mixture.[2]

Both Zacharias and Elizabeth were righteous and walked before God blamelessly. They were both very old and were in danger of not perpetuating their family line generationally when God chose them as the parents for John the Baptist. God seems to take pleasure in perpetuating His blessing in those who in the natural have no ability to do so. Abraham and Sarah were also blessed with a child of promise beyond the natural age of childbearing.

Matthew Henry's Commentary also says this about Zacharias,

Now the father of John Baptist was a priest, a son of Aaron; his name *Zacharias*. No families in the world were ever so honored of God as those of Aaron and David; with one was made the covenant of priesthood, with the other that of royalty; they had both forfeited their honour, yet the gospel again puts honor upon both in their latter days, on that of Aaron in John Baptist, on that of David in Christ, and then they were both extinguished and lost. Christ was of David's house, his forerunner of Aaron's; for his priestly agency and influence opened the way to his kingly authority and dignity.[3]

THE EARTHLY PARENTS OF JESUS

Now the birth of Jesus Christ was as follows: After His mother Mary was betrothed to Joseph, before they came together, she was found with child of the Holy Spirit. Then Joseph her husband, being a just man, and not wanting to make her a public example, was minded to put her away secretly. But while he thought about these things, behold, an angel of the Lord appeared to him in a dream, saying, "Joseph, son of David, do not be afraid to take to you Mary your wife, for that which is conceived in her is of the Holy Spirit. And she will bring forth a Son, and you shall call His name Jesus, for He will save His people from their sins."

So all this was done that it might be fulfilled which was spoken by the Lord through the prophet, saying: "Behold, the virgin shall be with child, and bear a Son, and they shall call His name Immanuel," which is translated, "God with us." Then Joseph, being aroused from sleep, did as the angel of the Lord commanded him and took to him his wife, and did not know her till she had brought forth her firstborn Son. And he called His name Jesus (Matthew 1:18-25 NKJV).

SKETCH OF JOSEPH

We know Joseph was not the real father of Jesus, but became an earthly guardian of Jesus. Jesus, being God incarnate, had no beginning and so was conceived supernaturally by the Holy Spirit in the virgin Mary. Joseph was a descendant in the line of David.[4] In Matthew 1:19 Joseph is called a *"just man."* God communicated with him through visions and dreams.

In Matthew 1:24-25, we see that Joseph believed what the angel of God told him about Mary and obeyed God by marrying her, but did not attempt a union with Mary until after the birth of Jesus. He was also a courageous man who would direct their hazardous journey to Bethlehem to comply with the Roman census (see Luke 2:1-7) and protect the King of kings, whose life would be in continual danger from Herod (see Matt. 2:1-2:23) and others like him until the angel of God again appeared and instructed Joseph to return to Nazareth.

SKETCH OF MARY

Now in the sixth month the angel Gabriel was sent by God to a city of Galilee named Nazareth, to a virgin betrothed to a man whose name was Joseph, of the house of David. The virgin's name was Mary. And having come in, the angel said to her, "Rejoice, highly favored one, the Lord is with you; blessed are you among women" (Luke 1:26-28 NKJV).

Mary was married to a man in the generational blessing of Messiah of the house of David. She was a holy woman of God, a virgin who kept herself pure. The angel of the Lord said she was *"highly favored"* of God and the Lord was with her.

> *And the angel said unto her, Fear not, Mary: for thou hast found favour with God. And, behold, thou shalt conceive in thy womb, and bring forth a son, and shalt call His name Jesus. He shall be great, and shall be called the Son of the Highest: and the Lord God shall give unto Him the throne of His father David: And He shall reign over the house of Jacob for ever; and of His kingdom there shall be no end. Then said Mary unto the angel, How shall this be, seeing I know not a man? And the angel answered and said unto her, The Holy Ghost shall come upon thee, and the power of the Highest shall overshadow thee: there-fore also that holy thing which shall be born of thee shall be called the Son of God. And, behold, thy cousin Elisabeth, she hath also conceived a son in her old age: and this is the sixth month with her, who was called barren. For with God nothing shall be impossible. And Mary said, Behold the handmaid of the Lord; be it unto me according to thy word. And the angel departed from her (Luke 1:30-38).*

Mary believed the Word of the Lord in spite of the natural impossibility of what was prophesied and obeyed in spite of how it could look to her betrothed, Joseph. *"Blessed is she who believed, for there will be a fulfillment of those things which were told her from the Lord"* (Luke 1:45 NKJV).

The generational blessing in Mary and Elizabeth's family must have been potent because Mary, the mother of the promised Messiah, and Elizabeth, the mother of John the Baptist, were cousins. God built a godly heritage through families for many generations in order for the plan of redemption to unfold in history through John the Baptist and the Lord Jesus Christ.

JESUS BUILDS THE CHURCH THROUGH FAMILY LINES

> *And when He had called unto Him His twelve disciples, He gave them power against unclean spirits, to cast them out, and to heal all manner of sickness and all manner of disease. Now the names of the twelve apostles are these; The first, Simon, who is called Peter, and Andrew **his brother**; James the son of Zebedee, and John **his brother**; Philip, and Bartholomew; Thomas, and Matthew the publican; James the son of Alphaeus, and Lebbaeus, whose surname was Thaddaeus; Simon the Canaanite, and Judas Iscariot, who also betrayed Him (Matthew 10:1-4).*

Of the 12 men Jesus chose as His disciples, the first four were sets of brothers! Moreover, three of the four, James, John, and Peter, became His inner circle that He poured into the most. Could it be that He built primarily with those who already had the most generational blessing behind them? We don't know much about the background of the apostles except to say that, looking at the biblical pattern, I wouldn't be surprised if most of them had some kind of godly line of blessing behind them.

JAMES, THE BROTHER OF JESUS

We don't have a lot of information on the half-brothers and half-sisters of Jesus in the biblical record, but Matthew 13 lists the names of the sons of Joseph and Mary and indicates that they had daughters as well.

> *Is this not the carpenter's son? Is not His mother called Mary? And His brothers James, Joses, Simon, and Judas? And His sisters, are they not all with us? (Matthew 13:55-56 NKJV)*

John 7:1-7 indicates that His earthly half-brothers did not believe Jesus during the time of His earthly ministry:

After these things Jesus walked in Galilee; for He did not want to walk in Judea, because the Jews sought to kill Him. Now the Jews' Feast of Tabernacles was at hand. His brothers therefore said to Him, "Depart from here and go into Judea, that Your disciples also may see the works that You are doing. For no one does anything in secret while he himself seeks to be known openly. If You do these things, show Yourself to the world." For even His brothers did not believe in Him. Then Jesus said to them, "My time has not yet come, but your time is always ready. The world cannot hate you, but it hates Me because I testify of it that its works are evil" (John 7:1-7 NKJV).

We do not have a biblical or historical record showing us in detail what happened to all of Jesus' half siblings, but we can tell you they became believers after the resurrection, and at least two of His half-brothers became very influential leaders in the early Church. It seems that all of Jesus' half-brothers were praying in the upper room with the other believers before the day of Pentecost.

*Then they returned to Jerusalem from the mount called Olivet, which is near Jerusalem, a Sabbath day's journey. And when they had entered, they went up into the upper room where they were staying: Peter, James, John, and Andrew; Philip and Thomas; Bartholomew and Matthew; James the son of Alphaeus and Simon the Zealot; and Judas the son of James. These all continued with one accord in prayer and supplication, with the women and **Mary the mother of Jesus, and with His brothers*** (Acts 1:12-14 NKJV).

James, one of His half-brothers, is mentioned in both the biblical record and in church history as the leader of the church in Jerusalem after Peter. Acts 12:16-17 says:

Now Peter continued knocking; and when they opened the door and saw him, they were astonished. But motioning to them with his hand to keep silent, he declared to them how the Lord had brought him out of the prison. And he said, "Go, tell these things to James and to the brethren." And he departed and went to another place (Acts 12:16-17 NKJV).

Paul counted James as one of the three pillars of the Jerusalem church, who along with Peter and John officially affirmed Paul's call to the Gentiles in Galatians 2:9-10:

When James, Cephas, and John, who seemed to be pillars, perceived the grace that had been given to me, they gave me and Barnabas the right hand of fellowship, that we should go to the Gentiles and they to the circumcised. They desired only that we should remember the poor, the very thing which I also was eager to do (NKJV).

And Galatians 1:18-19 says:

Then after three years I went up to Jerusalem to see Peter, and abode with him fifteen days. But other of the apostles saw I none, save James the Lord's brother.

James also presided as the leader at the first ever general council of the Church held in Jerusalem.

And after they had become silent, James answered, saying, "Men and brethren, listen to me: Simon has declared how God at the first visited the Gentiles to take out of them a people for His name. And with this the words of the prophets agree, just as it is written: 'After this I will return and will rebuild the tabernacle of David, which has fallen down; I will rebuild its ruins, and I will set it up; so that the rest of mankind may seek the Lord, even all the Gentiles who are called by My name, says the Lord who does all these things.' Known to God from eternity are all His works. Therefore I judge that we should not trouble those from among the Gentiles who are turning to God, but that we write to them to abstain from things polluted by idols, from sexual immorality, from things strangled, and from blood. For Moses has had throughout many generations those who preach him in every city, being read in the synagogues every Sabbath." Then it pleased the apostles and elders, with the whole church, to send chosen men of their own company to Antioch with Paul and Barnabas... (Acts 15:13-22 NKJV).

According to this narrative, James spoke the last official words concerning the vital question of whether or not Gentiles should keep the law of Moses in order to be saved. At stake was the very future of the Church! After James spoke, the apostles and the whole Church acted, inferring the word from James seemed to bring the discussion to a close. Thus, the early Church deferred to the biological half-brother of Jesus, even over the apostle Peter, because they respected the lineage and generational call on the biological family of Jesus.

JUDE, THE BROTHER OF JAMES

Finally, the author of the small letter located right before the Book of Revelation in the New Testament identifies himself in the very first verse; *"Jude, the servant of Jesus Christ, and brother of James, to them that are sanctified by God the Father, and preserved in Jesus Christ, and called"* (Jude 1). In the early Church, there is only one James who could be referred to in this way without further specification, and that was James, the Lord's brother. This Jude was probably the same one who is numbered among the physical brothers of the Lord Jesus in Matthew 13:55 and Mark 6:3. If the author of the Book of Jude is indeed one of the physical brothers of Jesus, then Jesus would have had at least two physical brothers that we know of who had powerful ministries that influenced the Church throughout history!

Jesus honored and was concerned for the well-being of His earthly family. Look at how He thought about His mother, Mary, even though He was about to complete the single most important event in the history of humankind and the universe.

> *Now there stood by the cross of Jesus His mother, and His mother's sister, Mary the wife of Cleophas, and Mary Magdalene. When Jesus therefore saw His mother, and the disciple standing by, whom He loved, He saith unto His mother, Woman, behold thy son! Then saith He to the disciple, Behold thy mother! And from that hour that disciple took her unto his own home. After this, Jesus knowing that all things were now accomplished, that the scripture might be fulfilled, saith, I thirst. Now there was set a vessel full of vinegar: and they filled a spunge with vinegar, and put it upon hyssop, and put it to His mouth. When Jesus therefore had received the vinegar, He said, It is finished: and He bowed His head, and gave up the ghost* (John 19:25-30).

JESUS BUILT THE CHURCH WITH A MULTIGENERATIONAL VIEW OF MINISTRY

In John 14:12, Jesus speaks of three things that show us His multigenerational view of ministry:

> *Verily, verily, I say unto you, He that believeth on Me, the works that I do shall he do also; and greater works than these shall he do; because I go unto My Father.*

The first generation He speaks of concerns the works He Himself was currently involved with. The second generation of ministry concerns the way the disciples were empowered to do the works He was doing while He was with them. The third generation and on concerns the corporate Church. Jesus foresaw His Church doing greater works than He did because He was with His Father.

Jesus further reiterates this multigenerational vision in what is commonly referred to as the Great Commission. In Mark 16, Jesus gives His final instructions to His disciples before being taken up into Heaven.

> And He said unto them, Go ye into all the world, and preach the gospel to every creature. He that believeth and is baptized shall be saved; but he that believeth not shall be damned. And these signs shall follow them that believe; In My name shall they cast out devils; they shall speak with new tongues; they shall take up serpents; and if they drink any deadly thing, it shall not hurt them; they shall lay hands on the sick, and they shall recover (Mark 16:15-18).

Then verses 19-20 confirmed the disciples did what they had been instructed to do, and that Jesus did indeed continue His work through them.

> So then after the Lord had spoken unto them, He was received up into heaven, and sat on the right hand of God. And they went forth, and preached every where, the Lord working with them, and confirming the word with signs following. Amen (Mark 16:19-20).

The Lord will continue to work through those who obey Him in each and every generation.

THINK ON THIS

No families in the world were ever so honored of God as those of

_____ and _____.

Mary, the mother of Jesus, was married to a man in the generational blessing of Messiah of _____.

God built a godly heritage through families for many generations in order for the plan of redemption to unfold in history through _____ and the Lord Jesus Christ.

Paul counted James, the brother of _____ as one of the three pillars of the _____ church, who along with Peter and John officially affirmed Paul's call to the gentiles in Galatians 2:9-10.

The author of the small letter located right before the Book of Revelation in the New Testament identifies himself as _____, which makes him the half-brother of _____.

What are the three things Jesus speaks of in John 14:12 that show us His multigenerational view of ministry?

_____

_____

_____

ENDNOTES

1. Matthew Henry, *Matthew Henry's Commentary on the Whole Bible: Complete and unabridged in one volume* (Peabody, MA: Hendrickson, 1991), Luke 1:5-25.

2. Ibid.

3. Ibid.

4. Note the genealogies of Christ in Matthew 1 and Luke 3:23.

CHAPTER 14

GENERATIONAL PROMISES IN THE BOOK OF ACTS

APOSTLE PAUL

PAUL studied under Gamalial, a teacher of the law who was honored by all people (see Acts 5:34-35), which illustrates to us the important influence his parents were in his life. Paul was brought up with a strong religious upbringing, made to study the law, and raised to be a Pharisee.

> He had a learned and liberal education. He was not only a Jew, and a gentleman, but a scholar. He *was brought up* in Jerusalem, the principal seat of the Jewish learning, and *at the feet of Gamaliel,* whom they all knew to be an eminent doctor of the Jewish law, of which Paul was designed to be himself a teacher; and therefore he could not be ignorant of their law, nor be thought to slight it because he did not know it. His parents had brought him very young to this city, designing him for a Pharisee; and some think his being brought up at the feet of Gamaliel intimates, not only that he was one of his pupils, but that he was, above

any other, diligent and constant in attending his lectures, observant of him, and obsequious to him, in all he said, as *Mary, that sat at Jesus' feet, and heard his word.* He was not trained up in the principles of the latitudinarians, had nothing in him of a Sadducee, but was of that sect that was most studious in the law, kept most close to it, and, to make it more strict than it was, added to it the traditions of the elders, the law of the fathers, the law which was given to them, and which they gave to their children, and so it was handed down to us. Paul had as great a value for antiquity, and tradition, and the authority of the church, as any of them had; and there was never a Jew of them all that understood his religion better than Paul did, or could better give an account of it or a reason for it.[1]

Paul must have had a love for the history and the traditions of Israel. Though his zeal was misguided, God saw that his passion for Him was genuine, and God was able to turn him around and use him mightily! Paul himself referred to his generational blessing in Second Timothy 1:3, *"I thank God, whom I serve with a pure conscience, as my forefathers did…"* (NKJV). Paul had at least two other relatives with an influential ministry who were of note among the apostles, as recorded in Romans 16:7. *"Salute Andronicus and Junia, my kinsmen and my fellow-prisoners, who are of note among the apostles, who also were in Christ before me."* In Romans 16:11, Paul greeted Herodian, another person in the Roman church he identified as his relative.

Paul's immediate family was sympathetic to his apostolic ministry, and God used his sister's son to save his life when he uncovered a Jewish plot to assassinate him in Acts 23:12-23:

> And when it was day, some of the Jews banded together and bound themselves under an oath, saying that they would neither eat nor drink till they had killed Paul. Now there were more

than forty who had formed this conspiracy. They came to the chief priests and elders, and said, "We have bound ourselves under a great oath that we will eat nothing until we have killed Paul. Now you, therefore, together with the council, suggest to the commander that he be brought down to you tomorrow, as though you were going to make further inquiries concerning him; but we are ready to kill him before he comes near." **So when Paul's sister's son heard of their ambush, he went and entered the barracks and told Paul. Then Paul called one of the centurions to him and said, "Take this young man to the commander**, *for he has something to tell him." So he took him and brought him to the commander and said, "Paul the prisoner called me to him and asked me to bring this young man to you. He has something to say to you." Then the commander took him by the hand, went aside, and asked privately, "What is it that you have to tell me?" And he said, "The Jews have agreed to ask that you bring Paul down to the council tomorrow, as though they were going to inquire more fully about him. But do not yield to them, for more than forty of them lie in wait for him, men who have bound themselves by an oath that they will neither eat nor drink till they have killed him; and now they are ready, waiting for the promise from you." So the commander let the young man depart, and commanded him, "Tell no one that you have revealed these things to me." And he called for two centurions, saying, "Prepare two hundred soldiers, seventy horsemen, and two hundred spearmen..."* (Acts 23:12-23 NKJV).

The fact that there were a number of his relatives in the faith is not a coincidence and probably shows that Paul was part of a godly family line with a powerful generational blessing.

FAMILY SKETCH OF TIMOTHY

In Acts 16:1-3, we see Paul meeting up with a young disciple named Timothy:

> *Then he came to Derbe and Lystra. And behold, a certain disciple was there, named Timothy, **the son of a certain Jewish woman who believed,** but his father was Greek. He was well spoken of by the brethren who were at Lystra and Iconium. Paul wanted to have him go on with him; and he took him and circumcised him because of the Jews who were in that region, for they all knew that his father was Greek* (NKJV).

Timothy's Jewish mother married into a Gentile family, and all of his religious background and generational blessing came from his mother's side of the family. Second Timothy 1:3-5 says he had at least two generations of training in the Scriptures prior to Paul, his grandmother Lois and his mother Eunice.

> *I thank God, whom I serve with a pure conscience, as my forefathers did, as without ceasing I remember you in my prayers night and day, greatly desiring to see you, being mindful of your tears, that I may be filled with joy, when I call to remembrance **the genuine faith that is in you, which dwelt first in your grandmother Lois and your mother Eunice, and I am persuaded is in you also*** (NKJV).

Timothy can also serve as a successful faith-building story to all mothers who attempt to nurture their sons in the faith in spite of the challenge of having an unbelieving husband. Timothy became the most effective disciple of the apostle Paul, which is a great tribute to his mother and grandmother! In Philippians 2:20, Paul says that of all his followers he had none like Timothy. This should also give hope to single moms everywhere that, with God's help, they can still successfully nurture their young sons in the Lord.

BARNABAS AND JOHN MARK

The apostle Barnabas was introduced in Acts 4:36 and was known to the early Church as the "son of encouragement." He was instrumental in supporting the poor saints in Jerusalem because he sold his land and gave the proceeds to the apostles. He was also a key person who had a hand in developing Paul the apostle by introducing him to the Jerusalem apostles in Acts 9:27. When news reached the Jerusalem church of converts in Antioch, they sent Barnabas to investigate. Then Barnabas sought out Paul, who was in Tarsus at the time, and brought him to assist in teaching the new Christians in Antioch (see Acts 11:19-26).

In Acts 12:25, we see Barnabas and Paul returning to Jerusalem and bringing Barnabas' cousin, John Mark, with them (see Col. 4:10). In Acts 13, we read of the tough missionary journey the three of them went on and John Mark's subsequent request to return to Jerusalem (see Acts 13:13). When Paul and Barnabas decide to go their separate ways, Silas accompanied Paul, and John Mark traveled with Barnabas.

John Mark later became an important figure as the spiritual son of the apostle Peter and perhaps the author of the Gospel of Mark. First Peter 5:13 shows his close relationship with Peter, and Church tradition teaches that the Gospel of Mark was really the oral account of Jesus dictated by Peter to Mark.

Thus we see how important both the biological family was in who God chose as apostles and also the important role spiritual parenting served with all these key New Testament leaders.

THE GENERATIONAL PROMISE

Therefore let all the house of Israel know assuredly, that God hath made the same Jesus, whom ye have crucified, both Lord and Christ. Now when they heard this, they were pricked in *their heart, and said unto Peter and to the rest of the apostles, Men and brethren, what shall we do? Then Peter said unto them, Repent, and be baptized every one of you in the name of Jesus Christ for the remission of sins, and ye shall receive the gift of the Holy Ghost. For **the promise is unto you, and to your children, and to all that are afar off**, even as many as the Lord our God shall call. And with many other words did he testify and exhort, saying, Save yourselves from this untoward generation (Acts 2:36-40).*

This passage teaches us that we are called to repent, be baptized, and receive the gift of the Holy Spirit and that this promised gift is also for our children and to all who are afar off. I used to think that *"to all that are afar off"* meant only geographic miles and that God wanted us to be missionaries. Close examination of this Scripture, though, tells us that it is not speaking of a geographic location, but many generations of our children! Another interesting aspect brought out in this passage is that by accepting this gift of salvation, we automatically cut ourselves off from this present perverse generation. The last verse instructing us to *"save yourselves from this untoward generation"* means from this "crooked, perverse, wicked, unjust generation."[2]

CORNELIUS

In the story of Cornelius, a centurion, God shows us His desire to reach not only everyone in our biological families, but also those we are in close relationship with and those who work for us.

There was a certain man in Caesarea called Cornelius, a centurion of the band called the Italian band, a devout man, and one that feared God with all his house, which gave much alms to the people, and prayed to God alway. He saw in a vision evidently about the ninth hour of the day an angel of God coming in to him, and saying unto him, Cornelius. And when he looked on him, he was afraid, and said, What is it, Lord? And he said unto him, Thy prayers and thine alms are come up for a memorial before God. ...And the morrow after they entered into Caesarea. **And Cornelius waited for them, and he had called together his kinsmen and near friends** (Acts 10:1-4,24).

And, behold, immediately there were three men already come unto the house where I was, sent from Caesarea unto me. And the Spirit bade me go with them, nothing doubting. Moreover these six brethren accompanied me, and we entered into the man's house: And he shewed us how he had seen an angel in his house, which stood and said unto him, Send men to Joppa, and call for Simon, whose surname is Peter; **Who shall tell thee words, whereby thou and all thy house shall be saved.** *And as I began to speak, the Holy Ghost fell on them, as on us at the beginning. Then remembered I the word of the Lord, how that He said, John indeed baptized with water; but ye shall be baptized with the Holy Ghost. Forasmuch then as God gave them the like gift as He did unto us, who believed on the Lord Jesus Christ; what was I, that I could withstand God?* (Acts 11:11-17)

Acts 12:1-18 records the account of the arrest of Peter by King Herod and how the home prayer meeting at the house of Mary the mother of John lifted up intercession for the apostle, which resulted in his rescue from the jailhouse.

Acts 16:13-15 records the salvation of Lydia and her family:

And on the Sabbath we went out of the city by a river side, where prayer was wont to be made; and we sat down, and spake unto the women which resorted thither. And a certain woman named Lydia, a seller of purple, of the city of Thyatira, which worshipped God, heard us: whose heart the Lord opened, that she attended unto the things which were spoken of Paul. And when **she was baptized, and her household,** *she besought us, saying, If ye have judged me to be faithful to the Lord, come into my house, and abide there. And she constrained us* (Acts 16:13-15).

Acts 16:25-34 shares the account of the jailer and his whole family who received salvation after God freed Paul and Silas from a Roman jail:

And at midnight Paul and Silas prayed, and sang praises unto God: and the prisoners heard them. And suddenly there was a great earthquake, so that the foundations of the prison were shaken: and immediately all the doors were opened, and every one's bands were loosed. And the keeper of the prison awaking out of his sleep, and seeing the prison doors open, he drew out his sword, and would have killed himself, supposing that the prisoners had been fled. But Paul cried with a loud voice, saying, Do thyself no harm: for we are all here. Then he called for a light, and sprang in, and came trembling, and fell down before Paul and Silas, and brought them out, and said, Sirs, what must I do to be saved? And they said, **Believe on the Lord Jesus Christ, and thou shalt be saved, and thy house. And they spake unto him the word of the Lord, and to all that were in his house. And he took them the same hour of the night, and washed their stripes; and was baptized, he and all his,** *straightway. And when he had brought them into his house, he set meat before them, and rejoiced, believing in God with all his house.*

Acts 17:2-7 reveals satan's number one plan for stopping the preaching of the Gospel by trying to destroy believing families:

And Paul, as his manner was, went in unto them, and three Sabbath days reasoned with them out of the scriptures, opening and alleging, that Christ must needs have suffered, and risen again from the dead; and that this Jesus, whom I preach unto you, is Christ. And some of them believed, and consorted with Paul and Silas; and of the devout Greeks a great multitude, and of the chief women not a few. But the Jews which believed not, moved with envy, took unto them certain lewd fellows of the baser sort, and gathered a company, and set all the city on an uproar, **and assaulted the house of Jason,** *and sought to bring them out to the people. And when they found them not, they drew Jason and certain brethren unto the rulers of the city, crying, These that have turned the world upside down are come hither also; Whom Jason hath received....* (Acts 17:2-7).

Acts 18:1-3 explains how the powerful husband and wife team of Aquila and Priscilla went into business with Paul and eventually ministered with him as well in Ephesus (see Acts 18:18-22).

After these things Paul departed from Athens, and came to Corinth; and found a certain **Jew named Aquila, born in Pontus, lately come from Italy, with his wife Priscilla;** *(because that Claudius had commanded all Jews to depart from Rome:) and came unto them. And because he was of the same craft, he abode with them, and wrought: for by their occupation they were tentmakers* (Acts 18:1-3).

When the local synagogue rejected the teachings of Paul:

He departed from there and entered the house of a certain man named Justus, one who worshiped God, **whose house was next door to the synagogue.** *Then Crispus, the ruler of the*

synagogue, **believed on the Lord with all his household.**
And many of the Corinthians, hearing, believed and were bap-
tized (Acts 18:7-8 NKJV).

Through these and many more examples throughout the New Testament, we can clearly see God continued the generational blessing shown
in the Old Testament. These blessings are still relevant today as God uses
the biological connections of family to accomplish His purposes!

BEWARE THE ENEMY'S TACTICS

Satan is well aware of the generational power and tried to contami-
nate a whole family by getting them to believe they could have power
over demons without an authentic relationship with Christ.

> *Then certain of the vagabond Jews, exorcists, took upon them*
> *to call over them which had evil spirits the name of the Lord*
> *Jesus, saying, We adjure you by Jesus whom Paul preacheth.*
> *And* **there were seven sons of one Sceva, a Jew, and chief**
> **of the priests, which did so. And the evil spirit answered**
> **and said, Jesus I know, and Paul I know; but who are**
> **ye? And the man in whom the evil spirit was leaped on**
> **them, and overcame them, and prevailed against them,**
> **so that they fled out of that house naked and wounded.**
> *And this was known to all the Jews and Greeks also dwelling*
> *at Ephesus; and fear fell on them all, and the name of the Lord*
> *Jesus was magnified. And many that believed came, and con-*
> *fessed, and shewed their deeds. Many of them also which used*
> *curious arts brought their books together, and burned them*
> *before all men: and they counted the price of them, and found*
> *it fifty thousand pieces of silver. So mightily grew the word of*
> *God and prevailed* (Acts 19:13-20).

As we conclude this chapter, I pray the Church will learn these truths and protect these principles in their families so we will see the next generation of church leaders and Christians take the Body of Christ to dimensions of greatness and cultural relevance only dreamed about by those of us alive today!

THINK ON THIS

What impact would the Body of Christ have on the world today if the principles of generational blessing were truly part of every Christian leader's lifestyle?

We would see:

- All "preacher's kids" serving the Lord.

- Mature third and fourth generation Christians leading the way in the Body of Christ and teaching us how to "seek first the Kingdom" without sacrificing the family!

- Christian youth keeping their faith all through high school and college!

- Sons and daughters of ministers of the Gospel taking the baton from their godly parents and continuing in their ministerial tradition like the faithful Levites of old churches and ministries involved in successful, multigenerational leadership transitions and transfers of ministerial grace and anointing.

What do we need to do to see this become a reality in our churches today?

_____

_____

_____

_____

_____

_____

ENDNOTES

1. Matthew Henry, *Matthew Henry's Commentary on the Whole Bible: Complete and unabridged in one volume* (Peabody, MA: Hendrickson, 1991), Acts.

2. James Strong, *Strong's Exhaustive Concordance to the Bible* (Peabody, MA: Hendrickson, 2009), entry #4646.

CHAPTER 15

DISCOVERING
THE GODLY SEED

It is not about nationalism, politics, or mere physical ancestry, but about God's purposes being perpetuated through His chosen seed. —Joseph Mattera

And I will put enmity between you and the woman, and between your seed and her Seed; He shall bruise your head, and you shall bruise His heel (Genesis 3:15 NKJV).

SINCE the fall of humanity, there arose two different seeds or generational lines in the earth. Genesis 3:15 articulates the two seeds and that there is enmity between the Seed of the woman, which represents the godly Seed leading up to Messiah, and the seed of the serpent, which represents the offspring of satan. Oftentimes Christians attempt to compromise with the world and think they can win. Enmity means there is hatred, hostility, and antagonism between the two seeds. In other words, it is a war. When there is a war, real peace only comes when one side obtains victory. A truce is usually short-lived and never engenders itself to true peace, as conflicts like those in the Middle East have repeatedly shown us.

ARE YOU IN THE LINE OF THE GODLY SEED?

The main thing we have to realize is not to get stuck on mere national, political, ethnic claims, or religious titles. Throughout Scripture, God makes it very simple to answer one very important question. Are you in the line of the godly Seed mentioned in Genesis 3:15, or are you of the seed of the serpent?

Jesus once created quite a stir because He told physical Jews that, although they were descendants of Abraham, they were not of His lineage because they didn't do the works of Abraham. He told them that their actions showed that their father was the devil!

> "I know that you are Abraham's descendants, but you seek to kill Me, because My word has no place in you. I speak what I have seen with My Father, and you do what you have seen with your father." They answered and said to Him, "Abraham is our father." Jesus said to them, "If you were Abraham's children, you would do the works of Abraham. But now you seek to kill Me, a Man who has told you the truth which I heard from God. Abraham did not do this. You do the deeds of your father." Then they said to Him, "We were not born of fornication; we have one Father—God." Jesus said to them, "If God were your Father, you would love Me, for I proceeded forth and came from God; nor have I come of Myself, but He sent Me. Why do you not understand My speech? Because you are not able to listen to My word. **You are of your father the devil, and the desires of your father you want to do.** He was a murderer from the beginning, and does not stand in the truth, because there is no truth in him. When he speaks a lie, he speaks from his own resources, for he is a liar and the father of it. But because I tell the truth, you do not believe Me. Which of you convicts Me of sin? And if I tell the truth, why do you not believe Me? He who is of God hears God's words;

therefore you do not hear, because you are not of God" (John 8:37-47 NKJV).

Matthew 12:33-35 also enlarges on the seed principle by saying that we are known by our fruit:

> *Either make the tree good, and his fruit good; or else make the tree corrupt, and his fruit corrupt: for the tree is known by his fruit. O generation of vipers, how can ye, being evil, speak good things? for out of the abundance of the heart the mouth speaketh. A good man out of the good treasure of the heart bringeth forth good things: and an evil man out of the evil treasure bringeth forth evil things.*

Being born into a Christian home is no guarantee that you will automatically be converted and exercise faith in Christ, just as being born in Israel did not make them children of Abraham. John 1:12-13 tells us that it is not flesh and blood that saves us; we have to be born of God.

> *But as many as received Him, to them He gave the right to become **children of God,** to those who believe in His name: **who were born, not of blood, nor of the will of the flesh, nor of the will of man, but of God** (NKJV).*

Even during the Old Testament period, not all of physical Israel was really of the seed of God. They had the Gospel preached to them through the types and shadows of Christ in the law and had to exercise faith in God to be saved, just like us in the New Covenant.

Romans 9:6-8 says:

> *But it is not that the word of God has taken no effect. **For they are not all Israel who are of Israel, nor are they all children because they are the seed of Abraham**; but, "In Isaac your seed shall be called." That is, those who are the*

children of the flesh, these are not the children of God;
but the children of the promise are counted as the seed
(NKJV).

Romans 2:28-29 clarifies this even further by saying:

For he is not a Jew who is one outwardly, *nor is circum-*
cision that which is outward in the flesh; but he is a Jew who
is one inwardly; and circumcision is that of the heart, in the
Spirit, not in the letter; whose praise is not from men but from
God (NKJV).

There is only one way to define *godly seed*. Are you in the line of the godly seed?

CHRONOLOGICAL SURVEY OF THE GODLY SEED

The following is a bit theological, replete with numerous biblical passages, but is necessary to track the godly seed through Scripture.

Genesis 1:28 originally shows us that the whole human race was in covenant with God through Adam. Genesis 3:15 shows us that after the Fall, the faith of God was passed down through the seed of the woman as opposed to the seed of the serpent and that the godly seed was at war against the seed of satan.

Genesis 5:1-3 shows the godly seed continued through Adam's son Seth. Genesis 9:1-2 shows the godly seed was preserved through Noah and re-given the original covenant of creation to bear fruit, multiply, and replenish the earth after the flood.

In Genesis 12:1-3, 15:1-6, 17:1-14, 18:10, and 22:17, Abraham becomes the father of all who believe and becomes the main person God uses to perpetuate the godly seed throughout history until the time of

Messiah. In Genesis 24:60 and 26:3-5, Abraham's son Isaac and Isaac's wife, Rebekah, continue the godly seed.

In Genesis 25:30-33, 27:19-29, 28:10-14, 32:22-28, and 35:9-12, Jacob is chosen to produce the physical nation of Israel and continue the godly seed. In Genesis 49:8-12, Judah is chosen as the specific family head of the tribe of Judah from which Christ was to descend.

Exodus 20:1-17 and Galatians 3:17-18, 24 explain that because of the transgressions in Israel, the Law of Moses becomes the "school master" for the nation to preserve the godly seed. In Deuteronomy 18:15, Moses is called a prototype of the coming Messiah and prophesies the coming manifestation of the godly seed.

In Second Samuel 7:12-13,16 and Luke 1:30-33, we see that David is chosen as the king from whom Jesus would descend. Galatians 3:16 and 4:4-5 declare that Jesus Christ, as the Messiah, becomes the fulfillment of the promised seed of the woman spoken of in Genesis 3:15.

Galatians 3:7-9, 13-14, 27-29, and Ephesians 2:11-19 explain that both believing Jews and Gentiles are now identified as the seed of Abraham and become one "new man" as the Body of Christ.

In Galatians 4:26,28,31, 6:16 and Hebrews 12:22, the entire Jewish/Gentile Church is now referred to in the Bible as *"Jerusalem which is above," "The Israel of God," "Mount Sion,"* and *"Heavenly Jerusalem."* As the Body of Christ, they are *in* the promised seed of the woman and consequently are now the carriers of the godly seed in the earth.

Revelation 21:1-7, 22:11 is the final consummation of the godly seed. Of course, the ultimate destiny of those numbered among the godly seed is to live throughout eternity in the presence of God. Conversely, the ultimate end of those who are of the seed of the serpent is to be eternally separated from God. This will result in eternal torment and the weeping and gnashing of teeth for those who chose the lineage of the ungodly seed (see Rev. 20:11-15; Mark 9:43-49; Matt. 25:30,41).

THINK ON THIS

This is a most important chapter in that the choice you make at this point determines whether you are of the lineage of the godly seed or that of the serpent. There is no middle ground.

Read John 3:16-21. What must you do to be saved from eternal separation from God?

_____

_____

Read Romans 8:1-17. How can we know we are children of God?

_____

_____

Read Galatians 4:4-7. Are you a slave or a son of God?

_____

Read John 8:31-47. Are you a child of God or a child of the devil?

_____

How do you know that?

_____

_____

You now have the responsibility to make sure the godly seed is perpetuated in your biological and spiritual children.

CHAPTER 16

HONORING SPIRITUAL FATHERS AND MOTHERS

If I honor those leaders who have paved the way for me, I will build my life upon the blessings they have incurred; but if I tear down those same leaders, I will attempt to build without a solid foundation, which will also greatly limit the heights I can attain. —Joseph Mattera

Children, obey your parents in the Lord: for this is right. Honour thy father and mother; which is the first commandment with promise; That it may be well with thee, and thou mayest live long on the earth (Ephesians 6:1-3).

WITHOUT a doubt, the number one hindrance to perpetuating a generational blessing in the Church is our disobedience to this commandment, especially in our Western culture that despises old age and glorifies youth. In the West, we glorify youth, physical strength, and appearance, and in the East they honor old age and the wisdom that accompanies it.

Hebrews 13:7 and 17 speak of those who have rule over you or that have watch over your souls. I believe this refers to the fifth commandment as it applies to our spiritual parents:

Remember *them which have the rule over you, who have spoken unto you the word of God: whose faith follow, considering the end of their conversation. ...**Obey** them that have the rule over you, and **submit** yourselves: for they watch for your souls, as they that must give account, that they may do it with joy, and not with grief: for that is unprofitable for you* (Hebrews 13:7,17).

The word *remember* in verse 7 speaks of honoring, loving, and blessing our spiritual parents for the lives they have lived in faith. The words *obey* and *submit* in verse 17 refer to allowing yourself to be accountable to your leaders, not resisting them and making it difficult for them to shepherd you and their flock.

As a local church overseer since 1984, I can't tell you how many times my heart has grieved when those with great potential never fulfilled their calling in Christ because they didn't honor or respect authority and didn't submit themselves to the leadership placed there by God. They chose to resist the corporate vision (see 1 Cor. 1:10) and caused division instead of unity in the house. Since these people didn't desire real accountability, they would run when they were confronted with their personal issues or when the leader attempted to bring them to a higher level of spiritual and emotional growth.

BREAKING THE FIFTH COMMANDMENT BY UNCOVERING OVERSEERS

There have been a number of instances in which I have heard of or been involved with a minister or a group of ministers that had issues with their covering or overseer. Unfortunately, instead of continuing to follow the principles set forth by Jesus in Matthew 18:15-17, they publicly uncovered the person in meetings, by letter, or in private conversations with other ministers who had no business being informed of the details.

These folks put themselves under the aforementioned curse of Ham in Genesis 9:20-27.

I have seen this curse work over and over again in numerous ministers and ministries; and in every one of them, their lives and/or their ministries fell apart or never ascended to the place of greatness originally planned by God!

In the late 1980s, I was tested with this very principle. At a very vulnerable time in my life, when my spiritual father moved out of town and I was left without a functional covering, I made the mistake of jumping into a relationship too quickly with a so-called apostolic leader. Within a year and a half, this overseer of mine went behind my back, lied about me to my elders, and attempted to wrest the church from me so he could take control of it. Thank God, the Lord moved in our behalf and revealed to me and my wife the seditious plot and gave us a strategy on how to counteract it. Without going into details, God gave us a great victory. The lies were uncovered, and I was vindicated by my elders. Neither then nor in the years since have I uncovered this unfaithful brother to my church. I only spoke openly to the elders who were affected and some spiritual leaders who helped walk me through this horrible experience.

I have also observed another way ministers sometimes break the fifth commandment. I remember one time eating lunch with a much-respected apostolic leader who is a dear friend of mine. As we were talking, he told me of a minister he sent out to plant a church almost 20 years ago. This leader told me he helped them with finances and training and even allowed some of the people in his congregation to become part of this church plant. Then, my dear friend, who has been in full-time ministry for about 50 years, put his head down, betraying the pain he still felt in his heart and said, "To this day, this person has never come back to thank me." When he said this, I also felt his pain. Consequently, the person he was referring to has gone through numerous church splits, has had leaders leaving and dishonoring him and many other troubles I can't detail here.

I can't help but think it is because he put himself under a generational curse by breaking the fifth commandment.

Remember, this commandment says that if you keep it, it will go well with you, and you will live long on the earth. The opposite is also true if you refuse to obey: It will not go well with you, and you will not live long on the earth. Applying the principles of the law of sowing and reaping, I believe this command can also apply corporately to a ministry. Breaking the fifth commandment explains why ministries don't have generational continuity.

In October 2000, my wife and I celebrated our 20th anniversary in full-time ministry. As part of our celebration, I asked my original pastor and first spiritual father to come and minister in our services. When the services were finished, my wife said to me that the day became an honoring service for my original pastor and not for us. When my wife said that, I was filled with joy and almost started crying because I felt so happy to be able to honor my first pastor. After all, if it wasn't for his life, his dedication, his vision for New York City, and his incredible anointing, I would not be where I am today in the ministry! I readily admit that the vision I have in my heart to love and minister to the city of New York is there because of Ben Crandall's preaching and 40 years of ministry in my region that prepared the way for me and other sons of his currently in the ministry.

I also knew that I was modeling to my elders and our spiritual sons and daughters how they should respect and honor me and my wife. I know, based on the law of sowing and reaping (see Gal. 6:7-9), that what I sow into someone else's life will come back to me. I knew that by honoring my original pastor and spiritual father, I was keeping myself and our ministry under a generational blessing and insuring success for years to come!

I also had another experience where my overseer was accused of wrongdoing in the ministry, and they attempted to discredit him and uncover him to numerous national leaders in the Body of Christ. My relationship with this person as my spiritual father transcended said accusations, and

I was forced to break relationship with a number of my close friends in the ministry. Knowing the details of the situation, I didn't think it had enough merit to break fellowship with my overseer. This overseer has since greatly advanced in the ministry and is now one of the most influential leaders in the world while those who uncovered him either died, repented, or have seen a great dissipation in their own ministries.

One of the leaders of the sedition went with another ministry and became second in command. I warned the leader of this other ministry that this person hadn't repented and would most likely do the same thing to him. Just a few years later, this leader and his wife were in a meeting with me and were greatly stressed because this same disloyal person was now positioning himself to try to take their ministry from them!

I have learned that every real relationship eventually passes through three stages: the Honeymoon stage, when everybody is excited about one another; the Disillusionment stage, when you find out about the foibles in the other person, and the immature or those who are just using you will leave you; and finally, the Reality stage, when the mature stick it out through the second stage into reality and stay there!

PARENTS FRUSTRATING THEIR CHILDREN

Ephesians 6:4 warns biological and spiritual mothers and fathers, *"provoke not your children to wrath: but bring them up in the nurture and admonition of the Lord."* I have seen many instances where pastors and spiritual leaders have stopped the generational blessing flow in the church by frustrating their spiritual children.

The "Saul and David" syndrome found in First Samuel 18:6-16 happens when insecure leaders won't allow the gifting of other leaders to develop because they feel threatened by emerging leaders and fear that they are after their jobs.

The "Bully Pulpit" syndrome happens when leaders use their pulpit to deal with individuals instead of confronting them one on one.

The "Impersonal Parent" syndrome describes leaders who only relate to their sons and daughters through their preaching and have little or no social interaction with them.

The "Lying Leader" syndrome frustrates spiritual sons and daughters because leaders break their promises and don't keep their word.

The "Congregational Chaos" syndrome is caused by leaders who don't manage the ministry properly.

The "Shifting Sands" syndrome frustrates spiritual children when leaders are constantly changing direction and pursuing new paths before the last vision is fully implemented.

The "Hypocritical Head" syndrome describes leaders who preach one thing, but do another thing.

The "Superficial Sell" syndrome leaders have style, but no substance in their plans to nurture emerging leaders; thus, there is no real follow-through or practical plan to process leaders to the next level.

Leaders with the "Lazy Leader" syndrome lack the passion, motivation, and drive in their ministry and frustrate younger, zealous leaders who want to use their gifts to focus on the mission of the church to reach cities.

Leaders with the "Lack of Praise" syndrome never affirm their spiritual children, but only correct them when they do wrong.

CONTRASTS BETWEEN FATHERS AND TEACHERS

For though ye have ten thousand instructors in Christ, yet have ye not many fathers: for in Christ Jesus I have begotten you through the gospel (1 Corinthians 4:15).

The Bible teaches us in First Corinthians 4:15 that we have many teachers, but not many fathers in the Church. During this day and age of hyper-feminism, it is important to remember the significant role fathers play in the formation of both their spiritual and biological children. I speak as a person who functions in and understands both roles. In most situations, when I am speaking outside of my local church, I function as a teacher. With pastors and leaders to whom I am assigned to oversee, I function more as a father with a teaching anointing. It is important that we understand the difference in the two roles if we are to perpetuate the godly seed.

1. Teachers disseminate information;
    fathers pour out their lives.

The primary function of a teacher is to take the revelation of Scripture and make it practically applicable for everyday living. While teachers are called primarily to spend time studying and dispensing knowledge and information, fathers are primarily called to pour out their lives to those for whom they are responsible. A father's primary method of teaching is through modeling excellence and wisdom in one's life for one's spiritual children. Fathers go by the adage "people don't care how much you know until they know how much you care."

This is the primary method Paul used to disciple Timothy, his foremost disciple. In a summation of his discipleship method, Paul reminded Timothy of "his way of life" right before his own martyrdom (see 2 Tim. 4:10-11). Paul defended his apostleship by illustrating his patient endurance in the midst of suffering, not by recounting his greatest sermons (see 2 Cor. 11:16-32). He was not only "spent" for his children, but he expended himself as well (see 2 Cor. 12:15).

2. Teachers are motivated by illumination;
   fathers are motivated by personal transformation.

As a teacher in the Body of Christ, I am constantly motivated to learn and understand more about the Scriptures and leadership principles so that I can pass my learning on through writing and preaching. However, when it comes to those I am assigned to father, I am more motivated by seeing the teachings bear fruit for personal transformation. I am called to walk with them, correct them, encourage them, and aid them in their life journeys so they will maximize their fullest potential. It is not enough for me to teach those in this group; I need to be available to coach them in their personal lives as well.

3. Teachers search for students;
   fathers search for sons and daughters.

Teachers enjoy nothing more than being in a room full of hungry students who can pull knowledge, information, and insight out of them. Those wired by God to father only view the classroom as an entree to find potential leaders they can have long-term connections with aid them in their journeys of becoming mature sons and daughters of Christ.

4. We have many teachers;
   we do not have many fathers.

Though there are countless teachers, mentors, and coaches in the Body of Christ who can edify all of us, each person is only assigned one primary father for their life's journey. For example, in biological families there is only one father and one mother, though a person may have grandparents, aunts, uncles, and siblings who impact his or her life.

I believe when Paul says this in First Corinthians 4:15, he is also referring to the fact that so few saints in the Church ever continue to mature enough in the faith so as to take on the role of a spiritual father. Through more than 30 years of full-time ecclesial ministry, I also concur that rare indeed is this function! How sad it is that most of the pastors and leaders in the Church try to replace the "way of Jesus and the apostles" with Bible institutes and schools. Formal Bible studies and education will never take the place of the model of nurturing leadership modeled in the Gospels, the Book of Acts, and the epistles. One of the reasons for so much disloyalty and splitting in the Church is the lack of fathering between senior pastors and their spiritual children. Children will have resentment and rebel against fathers who do not spend time with them.

I believe the primary reason many leaders in the Body of Christ die unsatisfied and unfulfilled is because when they look back on their lives, they see that they have not left behind a legacy of spiritual children who will carry on their work. Fame, speaking at large conferences, or writing best-selling books will never satisfy people in old age like having their children around them!

5. Teachers bask in joy at academic success; fathers enjoy life success.

Teachers are thrilled when their students do well in school and become great students of the Word. Fathers realize that just because someone is filled with knowledge and has a great grasp of biblical knowledge, there is no guarantee that person will have a successful personal life and fulfill their mission. John said that he had no greater joy than to find his children walking in the truth—not in his children merely having the truth (see 2 John 4; 3 John 4).

6. Teachers have an intellectual connection with their students; fathers have a heart connection with their children.

Teachers are stimulated when they have deep intellectual exchanges with students and congregations while teaching and preaching or while doing question and answer sessions during informal discussions. They walk away from such encounters extremely satisfied because of the opportunity to dispense their vast knowledge. Fathers are not satisfied with such exchanges unless they also involve a long-term strategy to pour their lives into their students. This is because fathers are motivated more by a heart-to-heart connection than an exchange of the minds. Heart-to-heart connections delve into the heart, the mind, the soul, and the emotions of a person. They enable a father to penetrate beyond the surface and into the real life of a son or daughter. While a teacher may get excited when a student screams amen during a great lecture, a father desires to peer into the compartmentalized life of a son or daughter with the intent to bring wholeness and integrity so that the teachings can bear much fruit and bring the children to maturity.

7. Teachers desire opportunity to teach; fathers seek opportunity for their sons and daughters to minister.

Teachers bask in the opportunity to teach, even to the point where they would do it for nothing if they had to! They are always looking for a platform to get out their vast knowledge through preaching, teaching, blogging, books, CDs, DVDs, and all other forms of available media. They gauge their level of success in life by how far and wide their teachings are being heard and received by the masses. On the other hand, fathers do not gauge their success by the extent of their ministry platform, but by the extent of the platform they prepare for their spiritual seed. They take greater pleasure being in the background while those they have poured into are bearing much fruit in the foreground! Instead of living for their 15 minutes of fame, they live to wash the feet of their children and commit their lives to their children's success!

8. Teachers are willing to teach a message; fathers are willing to live a message.

Finally, while many are attempting to preach and teach a message, not many are willing to live that message out through those they have spent years coaching into maturity. Oh God, give us more fathers!

CALLED TO RELATE ON THREE LEVELS

All pastors and leaders should have another to whom they personally submit. We must demonstrate to those under us, as the centurion did in Matthew 8:8-9, that we have earned the right to give orders because we have also learned to take orders. We all need to learn that God has called us to relate on three different levels to experience a full and healthy life.

We need to relate to our biological and spiritual children by pouring into them and raising them up to maturity. We need siblings we relate to as peers for fellowship, fun, and encouragement. We need parents we relate to for accountability, help, and impartation.

In closing, read the following words spoken by Job regarding the way a patriarch of old was respected by his contemporaries.

> *Moreover Job continued his parable, and said, Oh that I were as in months past, as in the days when God preserved me; when His candle shined upon my head, and when by His light I walked through darkness; as I was in the days of my youth, when the secret of God was upon my tabernacle; when the Almighty was yet with me, when my children were about me; when I washed my steps with butter, and the rock poured me out rivers of oil; when I went out to the gate through the city, when I prepared my seat in the street! The young men saw me, and hid themselves: and the aged arose, and stood up. The princes refrained talking, and laid their hand on their mouth. The nobles held their peace, and their tongue cleaved to the roof of their mouth. When the ear heard me, then it blessed me; and when the eye saw me, it gave witness to me: because I delivered the poor that cried, and the fatherless, and him that had none to help him. The blessing of him that was ready to perish came upon me: and I caused the widow's heart to sing for joy. I put on righteousness, and it clothed me: my judgment was as a robe and a diadem. I was eyes to the blind, and feet*

was I to the lame. I was a father to the poor: and the cause which I knew not I searched out. And I brake the jaws of the wicked, and plucked the spoil out of his teeth. Then I said, I shall die in my nest, and I shall multiply my days as the sand. My root was spread out by the waters, and the dew lay all night upon my branch. My glory was fresh in me, and my bow was renewed in my hand. Unto me men gave ear, and waited, and kept silence at my counsel. After my words they spake not again; and my speech dropped upon them. And they waited for me as for the rain; and they opened their mouth wide as for the latter rain. If I laughed on them, they believed it not; and the light of my countenance they cast not down. I chose out their way, and sat chief, and dwelt as a king in the army, as one that comforteth the mourners (Job 29:1-25).

See Appendix A: "Eight Reasons Men Reject Spiritual Fathers" for an addendum of this chapter.

THINK ON THIS

There are some key words in this chapter that we need to make sure we understand. Use both a dictionary and the Bible to define the following words.

Define *Honor:*

_____

_____

_____

What does it mean to honor your parents?

_____

What does it mean to honor those in authority over you?

Define *Obey:*

What does it mean to obey your parents?

What is the promise given in the fifth commandment concerning honoring and obeying your parents?

Does this commandment apply to your spiritual parents?

Define *Submit:*

_____

_____

_____

What does it mean to submit to those in authority over you?

_____

_____

How is this different from obeying those in authority over you?

_____

_____

Who are your spiritual parents?

_____

_____

Do you honor them as instructed in God's Word?

_____

_____

CHAPTER 17

MAXIMIZING THE BLESSING

His mercy is on them that fear Him from generation to generation (Luke 1:50).

I N this chapter, I give you some practical applications for what has been taught that will help you stay in the flow of your God-ordained generational blessing.

FOR INDIVIDUAL CHRISTIANS

Try to research your family tree, your genealogy. There are numerous genealogical tools you can find online by researching this topic. Find out if your family has an official emblem and the reason for the emblem. It may show something about the corporate purpose your family has had through the ages. If you are a second generation Christian or longer, you are most probably the beneficiary of a generational blessing. Do your best to walk in that blessing by honoring your father and mother. It would also be good to know the particular spiritual and natural giftings that were evident in your Christian ancestors. This should give you some understanding of what God may be calling you or your children to walk in.

If you are in a local church and sitting under a man or woman of God, understand that your faithfulness to them enables you to be under the corporate blessing of that church and also to be the recipient of the spiritual deposit of the leadership ministering to you!

Matthew 10:40-41 says:

> He that receiveth you receiveth Me, and he that receiveth Me receiveth Him that sent Me. He that receiveth a prophet in the name of a prophet shall receive a prophet's reward; and he that receiveth a righteous man in the name of a righteous man shall receive a righteous man's reward.

We receive grace according to the measure of the five-fold ministry gifting we are in submission to and sitting under.

> But to each one of us grace was given according to the measure of Christ's gift. Therefore He says: "When He ascended on high, He led captivity captive, and gave gifts to men." (Now this, "He ascended"—what does it mean but that He also first descended into the lower parts of the earth? He who descended is also the One who ascended far above all the heavens, that He might fill all things.) And He Himself gave some to be apostles, some prophets, some evangelists, and some pastors and teachers, for the equipping of the saints for the work of ministry, for the edifying of the body of Christ" (Ephesians 4:7-12 NKJV).

By connecting the context in verse 7 with verses 11 and 12, we see that the five "ministry gifts" mentioned are the vehicles God uses to dispense His grace in the saints for the purpose of equipping them for the work of the ministry. Therefore, it is not just you and God and your Bible acting out a "vertical relationship." It is you, God, and your faithfulness to God expressed in His Body horizontally that releases the anointing and maturity necessary for your ministry to be fulfilled.

If you have physical and spiritual children, be cognizant of the fact that the more obedient you are to the Lord, the more blessing you will release to your children. Realize that you are always a model for them, and what you do will exponentially multiply for generations.

Proverbs 14:26 says, *"In the fear of the Lord is strong confidence: and His children shall have a place of refuge."* Proverbs 13.22 says, *"A good man leaveth an inheritance to his children's children: and the wealth of the sinner is laid up for the just."*

Become a student of the Word and of church history so you can have more context for your life and a better appreciation for those who have gone before you.

Discover and learn how to break negative generational habits and patterns.

BREAKING GENERATIONAL CURSES

Review how your parents resolved conflicts, communicated, showed affection, handled stress, used their time, related to other family members and friends, suffered with sickness, mental illness, fears and phobias, pro-crastination, rebellion, drugs, false religions, and so forth.

Write down areas of your life, marriage, and family in which you carry over the wrong habit patterns of your parents or still suffer the effects of their sins and curses. Then confess and repent of these patterns with your spouse if married and break the curse over your family line in the name of Jesus.

Reveal to your children what you have been doing wrong and ask their forgiveness, asking them not to repeat the same patterns.

Establish a regular family altar. Husbands need to lead in family prayer and the reading of the Word, not just their wives. In the case of a single mom, as the spiritual head of her house, she will need to lead in this area.

A women married to an unsaved husband also has to take the lead spiritually until her husband comes to faith in Christ.

Understand that in most cases the model "house of God" will not be fully established in a first generation Christian family, but in their children's. Rarely do first-generation parents get it right in regard to having a house of the Lord. First Chronicles 28:2-3,6 shows that David could not build God a house because he was a man of war and much bloodshed, and that his son Solomon would be the one to build God a house and a resting place.

FOR LEADERS

Build on the generational blessings that are manifesting both in your family line and the history of your ministry. Go out of your way to publicly and privately honor those who have mentored you. Proactively get to know the older, seasoned ministers in your area who have paid the price in your region. Be an example of obeying the fifth commandment toward your physical and spiritual parents.

Become a student of church history and see how you can glean from this Body of Christ that the Holy Spirit has been building for over two thousand years. Be a student of biblical history and theology so you can better reflect the comprehensive plan of God in terms of your thinking, strategy, discipling, and word ministry.

Train yourself to think in terms of a minimum of three generations, because God identified Himself in history as the God of Abraham, Isaac, and Jacob. Avoid the current frenzied one-generational preaching employed by many ministers today. See how you and your church can be more involved in the community so that you can start to build a "community portfolio" that will give your ministry a greater platform for social relevance that will pay dividends in the years to come. Employ more than one strategy in terms of reaching your community for Christ. Don't just depend on the glory cloud coming down like so many have. Have a multigenerational plan of empowering the families and raising up the youth to take the lead in every facet of society.

Broaden your reading. Those who only read what is easy or what they feel comfortable with often stunt their growth. Acquaint yourself with some of the old Christian classics like, *Pilgrims Progress* by John Bunyan, *The Reformed Pastor* by Richard Baxter, *The Life Story of George Whitefield* by Arnold Dalimore, and many others. Other books that can motivate and inspire you include the autobiography of Charles Finney, the writings of St. Augustine, Calvin, and Jonathon Edwards, and the sermons of John Wesley and Charles Spurgeon. Some of the more contemporary writings, such as *Mere Christianity* by C.S. Lewis, *The Christian Manifesto* by Francis Schaefer, and N.T. Wright's *Simple Christianity* will give you a broader scope of what Christianity encompasses. By broadening your reading, you will broaden your mind, increase your discernment, and become a better minister of the Gospel.

LEAVE THE NEXT GENERATION A DOUBLE PORTION

Jesus said in John 14:12-14:

> *Verily, verily, I say unto you, He that believeth on Me,* **the works that I do shall he do also; and greater works than these shall he do***; because I go unto My Father. And whatsoever ye shall ask in My name, that will I do, that the Father may be glorified in the Son. If ye shall ask any thing in My name, I will do it.*

Elisha asked Elijah to give him a double portion so he could carry on God's work when Elijah was gone.

And it came to pass, when they were gone over, that Elijah said unto Elisha, Ask what I shall do for thee, before I be taken away from thee. And Elisha said, I pray thee, let a double portion of thy spirit be upon me. And he said, Thou hast asked a hard thing: nevertheless, if thou see me when I am taken from thee, it shall be so unto thee; but if not, it shall not be so. And it came to pass, as they still went on, and talked, that, behold, there appeared a chariot of fire, and horses of fire, and parted them both asunder; and **Elijah went up by a whirlwind into heaven. And Elisha saw it, and he cried, My father, my father,** *the chariot of Israel, and the horsemen thereof. And he saw him no more: and he took hold of his own clothes, and rent them in two pieces. He took up also the mantle of Elijah that fell from him, and went back, and stood by the bank of Jordan; And he took the mantle of Elijah that fell from him, and smote the waters, and said, Where is the Lord God of Elijah? and when he also had smitten the waters, they parted hither and thither: and Elisha went over. And when the sons of the prophets which were to view at Jericho saw him, they said,* **The spirit of Elijah doth rest on Elisha.** *And they came to meet him, and bowed themselves to the ground before him* (2 Kings 2:9-15).

SHOW GOD'S STRENGTH AND WONDERFUL WORKS TO THE GENERATION TO COME

Give ear, O My people, to My law: incline your ears to the words of My mouth. I will open my mouth in a parable: I will utter dark sayings of old: which we have heard and known, and our fathers have told us. We will not hide them from their children, shewing to the generation to come the praises of the Lord, and His strength, and His wonderful works that He hath *done. For He established a testimony in Jacob, and appointed a law in Israel, **which He commanded our fathers, that they should make them known to their children: That the generation to come might know them, even the children which should be born; who should arise and declare them to their children:** That they might set their hope in God, and not forget the works of God, but keep His commandments* (Psalm 78:1-7).

THINK ON THIS

In this chapter I gave you some practical applications of what has been taught that will help you stay in the flow of your God-ordained generational blessing. Go back through and highlight the ones you need to do as an individual and as a church leader. As you complete each one, also record the changes you see in yourself and in your generation as a result of your obedience.

CHAPTER 18

PERPETUATING THE BLESSING

Ye are the salt of the earth: but if the salt have lost his savour, wherewith shall it be salted? it is thenceforth good for nothing, but to be cast out, and to be trodden under foot of men. Ye are the light of the world. A city that is set on an hill cannot be hid. Neither do men light a candle, and put it under a bushel, but on a candlestick; and it giveth light unto all that are in the house. Let your light so shine before men, that they may see your good works, and glorify your Father which is in heaven (Matthew 5:13-16).

SINCE I take the theological position that the local church is the hope of the world as the salt and light, I believe that we need to address the turmoil in the nation and Church world because of economic and relational stress. There are many senior pastors who are about to leave the scene and many, if not most, are not ready to pass the baton to someone else! Some of the larger mega-churches have an even bigger issue on their hands when their senior leader steps down or retires if they can't find a leader with the gifts and charisma to fill their huge auditoriums.

Although many mainline denominational churches may last longer than one generation, there is no real intergenerational vision, which results in a maintenance mentality. This is one of the main reasons many denominational churches are small and ineffective in regard to community transformation. To rectify this situation, we need to understand the difference between the multigenerational and the one-generational mindset.

1. Multigenerational churches make leadership development their top priority. One-generational churches make Sunday services and programs their top priorities.

Churches with a multigeneration vision have learned to jettison all programs and ministries that do not ultimately result in either winning people to Christ or developing leadership. In Matthew 9:36-37, Jesus didn't tell His Church to pray for new converts, but for more leaders, because the harvest is already plentiful. Churches that develop a lot of leaders will always have church growth because they will have the capacity to handle new people attempting to assimilate. Churches that only care about "the now" will concern themselves with making it from one week to the next and are enraptured when they have a good Sunday service! A church that does not develop leaders has a slim chance of perpetuating its vision to the next generation when a "now" pastor leaves.

2. Multigenerational churches nurture spiritual sons and daughters of the house. One-generational churches merely nurture those with church membership status.

In multigenerational churches there is a vision for the leadership to personally pour into the lives of people in the church, especially those they select to disciple or mentor. The most effective way to nurture a multigenerational vision is to raise up loyal "sons and daughters" of the house who perpetuate the vision into the next generation. We see an example of how powerful the principle of nurturing people as part of your house is in Genesis 14:14-16, when Abraham defeats four nations with just 318 men trained and born in his house.

I have witnessed firsthand the blessing of having sons and daughters of the house who stand by me and our church through thick and thin and who never betray us. Some even call me dad and my wife mom because we poured not only the Gospel of Christ into them, but our very lives as well. It is these who will carry the vision to the next generation. These serve in the Kingdom of God with me the same way Elisha the prophet did with Elijah, whom he referred to as "my father" when he ascended into Heaven in a chariot of fire (see 2 Kings 2). These are the ones in whom God will bestow the Spirit so that they can serve with an even greater measure of grace than their leaders did before them!

3. Multigenerational churches employ the New Testament model of personal mentoring to nurture core leadership. One-generational churches depend on Bible institutes and seminaries.

The Hebraic style of leadership development was to have an apprentice spend time with you, learning from your teachings, but also from your way of life. This is the model that the Lord Jesus used to train the 12, and this is the primary model of the early Church, as exemplified in the apostle Paul and his disciple Timothy. It takes longer this way and is not as structured, but it is by far the most effective way to nurture world class leadership. Although this is clearly the method employed by Jesus, the apostles, and even the great leaders of the Old Testament, most pastors today depend upon a more formal, structured method like Church Bible institutes or some learning track that formally meets throughout the year.

Although this may be a great model for grounding the church in the Word, it can never take the place of the Hebraic model for effectiveness because human beings learn both academically and experientially. The greatest experience they will ever have in the Church is when they spend personal time with the senior leaders while they are actually doing the work of the Lord. Many of the most effective leaders I presently have in my church spent years living with me in my house or in an apartment they rented from me. This gave us ample access to one another and further accelerated the learning and maturing process.

4. *Multigenerational churches have an average congregational age between 25-40. One-generational churches have an average age of 50 and older.*

I have ministered in large churches that I am very concerned about because the average age of their congregation was 50 and above. Most likely, a church like this doesn't have an effective youth ministry, and they are losing all their young people to the world. I have also ministered in many vibrant churches that I know have a great future because the average age of their church was well under the age of 40. To give you an example of how this worked generationally in our local church, my youngest son Justin presently leads our youth group. He took the place of my spiritual son, Kristian, who lived with me for many years and led the youth. Kristian took the place of another spiritual son David, who started in our children's ministry at 9 years old and led our youth group for many years when he was in his 30s before handing it over to Kristian.

Our youth group is so powerful that many of the strongest preachers, teachers, and ministers of the Word are in their teens, and the most important ministers for our Sunday pulpit ministry and discipleship program are now only 30 years old. We already know that the next generation of our local church will be stronger than our present generation.

5. *Multigenerational churches have a compelling vision for the distant future. One-generational churches are merely on survival mode and are concerned with the immediate future.*

Churches with a multigenerational call have incorporated a vision that embraces a youth culture that will carry the church into the next generation. We are all called to have a vision that is so big it would be impossible for us to fulfill it in our lifetimes. It is meant to see its apex two to three generations into the future. Abraham's vision was so big that it wasn't until Jacob, his grandson, was born that the vision began to take shape. The vision for the formation of the nation of Israel led to the birth of Jesus and a multitude of nations coming to God as the seed of Abraham in Christ (see Heb. 11:13; Gal. 3:29).

One-generational churches have a vision for what they are accomplishing in the present time. Some even go so far as to financially mortgage the future for the present by getting into debt with large building projects that will not be sustainable for the next generation unless the building somehow miraculously gets paid off. Churches on course to last only one generation are only thinking in the short term and have no real plans past the next few local church events. Whatever God does is multigenerational, whether for our biological family, our businesses (see Prov. 13:22), or our churches. Therefore, all of our planning in these areas needs to be for at least three generations. When God revealed Himself to Moses, He called Himself the God of Abraham, Isaac, and Jacob (see Exod. 3). He is always revealing Himself to us in ways that cause us to think past our present generation to the generation of our children's children.

6. Multigenerational churches focus their target audience on their changing community demographics. One-generational churches remain focused on the same ethnic and economic group decade after decade.

When I first came to Sunset Park Brooklyn to minister in the early 1980s, there were numerous Norwegian churches in the area that were getting smaller and smaller. By the mid 1980s, all their church buildings had to be sold to either Hispanic or Chinese congregations who were moving into the community. The Norwegian Christians only had a vision for their own ethnic people, so they became irrelevant once the immigration from Norway to New York slowed down to a trickle.

Local churches that want to thrive from one generation to the next have to continually study the changing demographics of their community. They need to devise strategies to win new ethnic groups to Christ and also develop them as leaders so the church leadership has a public face that represents the ethnic milieu of their community. Churches that fail to do this will only last one generation.

Last year I spoke to a group of black pastors in Harlem and told them that because of gentrification, Harlem is being populated more and more with educated, Caucasian yuppies. If these churches want to have a future and be relevant in the next decade, they are going to have to reach some of these white folks and assimilate them into their church leadership. I would hate to go to Harlem in ten years and find a large number of these black churches closed down or sold to other congregations because they dwindled too much to financially sustain themselves.

7. Multigenerational churches are continually expanding their governing board to include younger leaders who will bear the burden. One-generational churches have small, aging boards who want to maintain power until they are in the grave!

Churches with a multigenerational vision will have younger leaders in as many eldership-related or planning meetings as possible. I try to explain all the things I am thinking and planning to my younger emerging leaders because I know they will be overseeing the church in the next decade. I also allow them to see how I act, pray, and problem-solve when in the midst of a great challenge or crisis so that they will be ready when it is their season to lead. Even if you don't make people under 30 official governing elders, you can still do a lot of things to empower them to lead a church by bringing them into your inner circle.

One-generational churches keep the same aged men in power decade after decade and never expand their governing base until it is too late! This frustrates the younger leaders who cherish the privilege of sitting at the feet of the more experienced, older leaders, especially when they are navigating the congregation through a crisis, a building project, or a vision implementation. One-generational churches become more and more irrelevant as the decades go by. Multigenerational churches keep in step with the times and the seasons of society and continually harness the energy, passion, and abilities of their young, emerging leaders.

8. Multigenerational churches have prophetic senior leaders who adjust their methodological approaches based on what God is doing from one decade to the next. One-generational churches have senior leaders who are stuck in the leadership style and methodologies of the distant past.

I have been in numerous conferences in which the theme and strategies were like something I heard in the late 1970s. It is almost as if these leaders are stuck in some decades-old mental time warp and their thinking preempts their ability to get into the 21st century Church! Those who are trying to reach their community the same way they attempted to reach it 30 years ago are not going to have success. The old axiom is "the message of the Gospel should always be the same, but the methods should always change based on your audience and the cultural times and seasons."

There are leaders preaching messages in which they are attempting to answer questions no one is asking instead of scratching people where they itch. Jesus spoke to the people based on their culture and vocation. When He was with fishermen, He told them He was going to make them fishers of men (see Mark 1:17). When He was with farmers, He spoke about the "sower sowing seed" (see Mark 4).

Multigenerational leaders have a prophetic bent in which they are able to discern the times and the season in which they live and, thus, articulate the message and strategize in a way that is relevant to their community and context. Prophetic leaders are the only leaders who will be able to navigate their congregations into the next generation with effectiveness. I know of one pastor who started his congregation in his home during the Catholic Charismatic revival of the mid-1970s. So many people came to Christ they had to start meeting in a church building, and they grew to about 200 people. Thirty years later, they are in the same building and have the same number of people because they never changed their approach. Their congregation is getting older, and what was once good enough for a revival is now going to serve as their graveyard if they don't make radical changes ASAP!

9. Multigenerational churches articulate the Gospel based on a comprehensive understanding of the culture and context of the society

they are immersed in. One-generational churches attempt to answer questions no one is presently asking.

The senior leaders of multigenerational churches hold the Bible in one hand and the newspaper in the other. They understand that as the sons of Issachar in First Chronicles 12:32, they are called to exegete culture as well as Holy Scripture. They read newspapers to see what is happening both nationally and locally so they can apply a biblical worldview to life and culture when they preach. Leaders who faithfully speak to the issues of the day in a language that relates to their audience and community will always have an influx of visitors who are hungry for the Word of God.

In Matthew 9:37, Jesus told us that "the harvest is plentiful" and that there will never be a shortage of people hungry to hear the Word. Like skilled fishermen, we know that the ocean is filled with fish, but we need the right bait to reel them into the boat. The right bait is a combination of preaching relevant messages and having a church culture conducive to church growth. By "culture" I mean being aware of the way people in the congregation dress, act, and think and projecting a spirit of excellence in ministry, appearance, and leadership. Leaders must have a heart for the sheep and accept people the way they are without putting human-made rules and regulations on them that become stumbling blocks to the reception of the Gospel.

Every Sunday I bring news stories related to sports, pop culture, and other areas of interest to the general population that I use to illustrate my sermons. This shows the people that I am down to earth and can relate to them on an emotional and intellectual level so I can connect the Word to their hearts. I also try to spend as much time as I can talking to our church attendees so I can have an idea of the struggles they are going through. This makes me a more effective communicator. Pastors who are not well-versed in pop culture, sports, and current events and who just preach out of stories found in the Bible will not be able to connect as easily to the average person.

10. Multigenerational churches have powerful, discipleship-oriented youth ministries, as opposed to youth ministries based on entertainment and socializing. One-generational churches have ineffective youth groups and are losing their youth to the world.

Perhaps the greatest sign that a church has a bright, multigenerational future is if they have a vibrant, discipleship-based youth ministry. I am referring to youth groups that have small group mentoring, strong, uncompromising preaching, high standards for dating, and a viable plan to serve their community and reach the lost. Youth groups that do not have a strong discipleship culture will most likely have a gathering based on entertainment and socializing, which will quickly devolve into a haven for sex, drugs, and chaos. I know a number of pastors with large churches who have shut down their youth ministries because it was actually hurting their church more than helping it due to the scandalous behavior of their attendees. Without a strong emphasis on the Word of God, a youth group can quickly get out of control and rip apart a local church in ways that will take years to rebuild.

Churches that either have no youth group or a youth group based on fun and games have no future and will only be one-generational. The only exceptions are churches that have successfully integrated their children and youth into the life of their adult congregation because their young people are able to understand the preaching at a young age. Churches like this are generally not large congregations, but nonetheless are successful in passing on their biblical faith to the next generation.

Throughout our congregational history, we have always had a strong emphasis on discipling our youth. We encourage our youth to participate in the intense, on-the-street inner city mission teams through music and drama or the "Acts Internship" project, which is supported primarily by a businessperson in our church and led by my youngest son Justin. This internship is perhaps the most powerful discipleship tool we have ever employed in our church and has helped us nurture a number of teens who can powerfully preach and teach the Word.

We now have a preaching rotation of these teens who preach in our Friday night youth sessions, run small groups, and occasionally even preach on a Sunday to our adult congregation. Ministries like this show me more than anything else I have ever been involved in that all of my labor in the Lord has been worthwhile. I know that our church is secure for generations to come!

11. Multigenerational churches emphasize strong marriage and family. One-generational churches only care about outreach and church performance and don't prioritize family or family ministry.

I have been married for more than 30 years and have functioned as a senior pastor for over 27 years. Through all this, I have come to the conclusion that an effective marriage ministry is absolutely essential for every church to succeed in its vision and purpose. Strong marriages are key if we are going to have stable young people in our church who will be able to have their own functional families and lead the church in the future. The key to having stable youth is to have strong, stable marriages.

Since churches are families of families, strong marriages are the foundation of the local church. Every local church is really a network of numerous families. Hence, the church is a macro expression of the micro nuclear family. Consequently, the macro health of the church is significantly dependent upon the micro health of each married couple that comprises a local church. The stronger the marriages are in a local church, the more significant commitments you will get from the husbands, wives, and children when it comes to volunteering time for lay ministry because they will have less personal and emotional distractions. The stronger the marriages, the more finances will come forth because families give more to those who invest in their health. Also, strong marriages mitigate against the high cost and financial ruin that accompanies divorce.

Strong marriages produce emotionally stable youth who ensure the future health of the church. Statistics prove that the children of fathers and mothers committed together in traditional marriage have greater emotional, physical, financial, and spiritual health. It is much harder to disciple young people from fragmented families because they don't have a model for spiritual authority, which in turn negatively affects their social functionality and local church commitment. Youth from divorced families are more prone to replicate the sins of their parents and experience divorce and fragmentation when they marry and have their own families. Instead of perpetuating stability and prosperity, they perpetuate the cycles of poverty and social dysfunction.

Strong marriages release the fullness of God's image in the church. Genesis 1:27 teaches us that God made both male and female in His image. Consequently, this passage implies that it takes both a male and female working together to demonstrate a more complete expression of who God is in a family and society. The most powerful and significant expression of male-female unity is the one flesh relationship experienced in marriage. Married couples in ministry have the potential to express the image and character of God more completely than just a man or a woman heading up or serving in a ministry.

Strong marriages model the Gospel to our community. It is a great witness for the un-churched when they see a low divorce rate in a community church. A church like this can become a haven for troubled marriages in the community. Ephesians 5:22-32 teaches that the covenant of marriage symbolizes the sacrifice Christ made on the cross to save humanity from our sins, so it can become a platform from which to preach the Gospel.

Strong marriages teach biblical stewardship in every aspect of life. Marriage and raising children are the greatest privilege and most demanding things most people will ever attempt. People usually do not experience the full essence of self-sacrifice, agape love, and commitment until they get married. If we fail to prioritize and provide for our families, First Timothy 5:8 says we are worse than infidels. Marriage is the greatest training ground for nurturing mature, well-rounded Christians and even world-class leaders for generations to come! See Appendix B for "Eight Practical Marriage Enrichment Strategies."

THINK ON THIS

Going from being a one-generational to a multigenerational church involves honestly looking at the way your church family is functioning. Go back through this chapter and highlight those areas that you now see need to be worked on in your church family so that you can move from being a one-generational to a multigenerational church.

Make a list below of what needs to be done; strategize with your church leaders, and develop a plan to begin implementing the changes needed.

_____

_____

_____

_____

_____

_____

_____

EIGHT REASONS MEN REJECT SPIRITUAL FATHERS

WE are all aware there is a dearth of fathers in our land that is cursing our American civilization. The millions of men in prison confirm this. An overwhelming majority of them have never had a normal relationship with their biological fathers.

Men in general are wired by God to achieve great things, but to also receive their father's affirmation for their accomplishments. The drive for a father's approval is so great that some men have responded to fatherlessness by engaging in destructive, addictive behaviors and/or becoming workaholics in attempts to accomplish great things to somehow fill the vacuum left in their fatherless hearts.

It is no different in the Body of Christ. God has raised up the Church as a family of families that can provide spiritual fathers and mothers who become surrogate parents helping to heal the pain of rejection in the hearts of their spiritual children.

Perhaps the greatest need we have in the Church today is for pastors and leaders to go beyond their professional titles and become relationally involved as spiritual parents with the people under their pastoral care. With the incredible breakdown of the American family, the Church is now the only hope to restore the vacuum left in the hearts of the fatherless in society.

However, I have also noticed there are men who refuse to allow spiritual fathers the emotional access necessary to nurture them. The following are reasons why some men reject spiritual fathers:

1. MEN REJECT SPIRITUAL FATHERS BECAUSE THEY NO LONGER TRUST MALE AUTHORITY FIGURES.

When young men experience abandonment from their biological fathers—whether physically or emotionally—they are usually nurtured emotionally by their mothers. This seems acceptable while a child is young, but once a boy reaches 11-12 years old, he will begin to act out and give his single mother much trouble. A father's abandonment leaves permanent emotional scars that can only be healed by God through forgiveness, our heavenly Father's love and acceptance, and by receiving a spiritual father into one's life.

Men who were abandoned by their biological fathers grow up not trusting male figures and tend to gravitate toward female authority—even to the point of receiving spiritual mothers while not trusting spiritual fathers. For example, I have always thought it interesting to see male athletes interviewed on television or radio since, most of the time, they thank God for their mothers and make no mention at all of their fathers.

2. MEN REJECT SPIRITUAL FATHERS BECAUSE THEY DON'T WANT TO BE HELD ACCOUNTABLE.

Some men are used to being independent because their biological fathers were so uninvolved that they grow up emotionally immature and—even though they may be past 30 years old—are still little boys emotionally. They still want to do their own thing and refuse to be corrected by anyone.

3. MEN REJECT SPIRITUAL FATHERS BECAUSE THEY ARE AFRAID OF BEING DISAPPOINTED.

A father's affirmation—whether biological or spiritual—is the most powerful experience a man or boy can ever have outside of God the Father's affirmation. When a man receives a spiritual father, he opens up his heart, emotions, and soul to this surrogate authority figure.

Because of this, spiritual fathers need to understand that just one word spoken out of place regarding their spiritual son's abilities, value, or worth can emotionally devastate and destroy him. So great is the power of a spiritual father's words that many men refuse to accept spiritual fathers because they do not want to take the chance of being hurt or rejected again by another person to whom they have entrusted their heart.

I have told spiritual fathers about the importance of their words—especially to men. It is very important to constantly tell men under your pastoral care (even older men) that you love them and are proud of them. Spiritual fathers *must understand the power of their words to their sons—that death and life are in the power of their tongues* (see Prov. 18:21).

I have witnessed firsthand men in leadership who try to serve in the ministry without a father's approval (whether spiritual or biological). They are driven, never satisfied, and even become abusers and manipulators of those who are under their care. They love and accept men as long as they are useful to their ministry, but they do not know how to father and love their sons unconditionally.

Hence, fatherless men produce fatherless sons in the Lord.

4. MEN REJECT SPIRITUAL FATHERS WHEN THEY HAVE SUFFERED ABUSE.

Men who have suffered verbal or physical abuse at the hands of their biological fathers tend to mistrust spiritual fathers and authority.

Our brains are trained to make associations with either pain or pleasure based on our upbringing. An abused son will associate all father figures with pain and abuse. Thus, they will tend to shy away from spiritual fathering until they are healed of their past.

Also, some men have experienced pain in the Church when so-called spiritual fathers have used them for their own advantages and abused or neglected them. If this occurs in someone's first experience with a spiritual father, they will tend to mistrust all future spiritual fathering, even if they come across a leader with the right heart and motive toward them.

5. MEN REJECT SPIRITUAL FATHERS BECAUSE THEY EXPECT PERFECTION FROM THEM.

Sometimes men act like little boys by placing their biological fathers on a pedestal and believing they are perfect in every way. I learned a long time ago that all people have sinned and fallen short of the glory of God (see Rom. 6:23). Even great leaders and spiritual fathers have character flaws and foibles. When men place their spiritual fathers on a pedestal, they are setting themselves up for great disappointment because no man has ever lived a perfect life except the Lord Jesus Christ. We need to understand that no matter how great a spiritual father, pastor, or leader may be, only Christ is perfect and is able to meet all of our spiritual and emotional needs.

6. MEN REJECT SPIRITUAL FATHERS BECAUSE THEY ARE AFRAID OF REJECTION.

When a man experiences a perceived rejection from a spiritual father figure, it is hard for him to start all over and trust another father figure, even if the rejection was only perceived and not real. Since many men would rather "go it alone" than face the pain of rejection, they never allow themselves to enter into that type of relationship again with another man.

For example, I know of men who will only let me get close to a certain point. Then they recoil and leave the church or back away from me because they can't handle the emotional intimacy of letting their hearts go past superficial religiosity and church attendance. Men like this need to risk being hurt again and trust the father figures God sends into their lives so they can be restored into full functionality and reach their potential in the Kingdom of God.

7. MEN REJECT SPIRITUAL FATHERS BECAUSE THEY DON'T KNOW THEIR HEAVENLY FATHER'S LOVE.

Men who are not secure in the love of God the Father will never be anchored enough emotionally and spiritually to be secure in any other relationship. To the extent that we experience the love, security, and affirmation of the love of God as our Father, to that extent will we be able to mimic that relationship with our biological father, spiritual fathers, and even be a good father to our own children.

8. MEN REJECT SPIRITUAL FATHERS BECAUSE THEY HAVE NEVER MET ANY AUTHENTIC ONES.

Unfortunately, the dearth of fathers has spilled over into this generation of Church leadership. We now have many pastors (both old and young) who don't know how to truly function as a father. Thus, we have few functional spiritual fathers. Evidently it was the same in the early Church: Paul says that we have many teachers, but not many fathers (see 1 Cor. 4:15). We cannot have what was never modeled for us or taught to us.

Many men I know have never had access to a pastor or a spiritual father. Many churches try to substitute personal fathering and mentoring with Bible institutes and classes, which produce spiritual children. This is as dysfunctional as parents who depend on public school teachers and day-care workers to provide all of the emotional support their children need in their formative years.

Overall, many men reject the pseudo-fathers in the Church because deep inside they know they are not authentic in their relationships. Since fathering is not an exact science, I have no barometer as to what constitutes true fathering in regard to the amount of quality time spent with an individual spiritual son. (We are all pressed for time and try to do our very best.) But I do know that a few of the "musts" for a true father-son relationship to develop include the following: There must be access, personal interaction when needed, regular input received, accountability, correction, affirmation, partnership in the ministry, and even friendship.

Because fathering is so involving, a leader cannot practically father more than 8-12 people at a time. But nowadays, because of technology with things like Facebook, texting, cell phones, emails, and so forth, spiritual fathers can certainly stay in touch with more men today than ever before. Thus, there is no excuse for not having regular contact with those spiritual sons God has placed in our paths.

Finally, because of the cultural decline of marriage, family, and the fragmentation of families related especially to the absence of biological fathers in the home, the local church must take the lead. We must be counter-cultural and develop a community model of family and spiritual parenting that the world can latch onto so that men can be healed, get married, have functional families, and become the biological and spiritual fathers that the world is waiting for. Otherwise, society will receive the full impact of the curse found in Malachi 4:6.

This teaching was taken from my leadership Website, www.josephmattera.org.

EIGHT PRACTICAL MARRIAGE ENRICHMENT STRATEGIES

1. PLAN AT LEAST ONE ANNUAL MARRIAGE ENRICHMENT EVENT.

It is amazing that most churches do not have even one annual event to edify married couples. Just starting off by planning an annual seminar or marriage retreat will go a long way toward preventing divorce and strengthening marriages.

2. HAVE A CONTINUAL PROGRAM FOR ENGAGED, TROUBLED, AND STRONG MARRIAGES.

A leadership couple in our local church developed an eight-week curriculum for a ministry in our church called Marriage Builders that we utilize for engaged couples, marriages in trouble, or for couples who want to improve their relationship. We are not aware of one divorce during the first 25 years of our church's existence among our members and committed attendees. (Of course, I am sure that a small handful have fallen away, left our church, and divorced.) Having a regular program or support group creates a culture of marriage enrichment and commitment in the local church context. Not doing anything for marriages creates a culture that acquiesces to the cultural diminution of marriage. Couples need a forum in which they hear what other couples are going through and also to keep open the lines of communication between themselves as husband and wife. Couples also need a forum in which sensitive and/or practical topics are unpacked objectively by an outsider who can speak truth to them without worrying about excessive baggage and issues that inhibit husbands and wives from speaking about such things.

3. DEVELOP MENTOR COUPLES TO EMPOWER THE LAITY AND RELIEVE THE LOAD OF THE PASTORAL STAFF.

Merely having a support group or marriage counseling is not enough.

The ultimate goal of all marriage ministries should be to equip and produce competent (but not perfect) couples that can coach and/ or mentor other couples dealing with the same issues they overcame in their marriages. For examples: step-family issues, interracial issues, special needs children issues, second marriage issues, financial issues, abuse issues, and so forth. Each mentor couple should specialize in ministering to another couple according to compatibility regarding the issues stated.

Mentor couples drastically reduce the counseling workload of the pastoral staff, which will release them to focus on other important issues. Producing mentor couples also fulfills the mandate in Ephesians 4:12, which teaches the Church to equip the saints for the work of the ministry.

4. HAVE PARENT EMPOWERMENT
SESSIONS TO AID THE COUPLES WITH CHILDREN.

The pressures related to raising children can be the most destabilizing factor for married couples. Regular sessions that empower good parenting enable parents to learn from trained experts in this field and also to learn from one another. This can also result in parents supporting one another with child care, prayer, and encouragement. Parent empowerment sessions take away another major stress factor that often divides instead of unites married couples.

Our church partners with a professional group of Christian psychologists who produce videos that a church facilitator can show and utilize for open discussion. (Thus, we don't need a parenting expert on site to run this program.) We also do parenting solutions sessions once per month for people in our community who are not members of our church. This has proved to be an amazing tool for getting the Gospel out to our community!

5. GIVE A FOCUS SURVEY
TO ALL ENGAGED COUPLES.

Marriage Savers utilizes a focus survey that is so effective that an average of 25 percent of all engaged couples cancel their wedding plans because they see their incompatibility based on salient questions the survey asks. Doing this presents a grid that can prevent marriages that will end in divorce, thus lowering the divorce rate.

6. REQUIRE A MARRIAGE
COUNSELING PROCESS BEFORE
THE CHURCH AGREES TO MARRY ANYONE.

In our local church, we generally require all engaged couples to take our eight-week marriage builders sessions before we agree to marry them.

Marriages without true preparation have less of a chance of lasting. Community marriage covenants always include this point as part of lowering the divorce rate in their region.

7. STAND UP FOR BIBLICAL MARRIAGE IN YOUR STATE.

All pastors and leaders need to stand up for traditional marriage and oppose alternate forms of marriage because strong marriage commitments require cultural cooperation. The erosion of the definition of marriage will also erode what is taught as the norm in public schools, universities, and health care. We need to avoid what happened when the Supreme Court ruled in favor of abortion with Roe vs. Wade, when most of the country was against abortion and the change in law resulted in more than one million abortions per year since 1973 to the present!

The redefinition of marriage will lower the cultural respect for traditional marriage, resulting in the lowering of the marriage rate and the acceleration of the cohabitation rate among unmarried couples. All of this will significantly hurt the standard of marriage in all our local churches nationally. (Unfortunately, after almost ten years of standing up for traditional marriage in New York State, same sex marriage was legalized by the State legislature in June 2011. With the help of an ad hoc New York State-wide coalition I put together for several press conferences and rallies, there is now a long political process to getting the State legislature changed to allow the people to vote as a state referendum on same sex marriage.)

8. TEACH COURTSHIP AND DATING IN LOCAL CHURCH YOUTH GROUPS.

This teaching will help prevent unwanted pregnancies and unhealthy relationships, which can stop the problem before it even arises. Preparation for marriage really starts when people are children through observing their parents' marriage model and by how they conduct themselves sexually when dating as teenagers. Included in these teaching sessions should also be: the emotional and physical consequences of having sex outside of marriage (including STDs, abortions, and rejection and emotional trauma) and the reality that choosing an incompatible marriage partner could wreak havoc on them for the rest of their lives!

HOW TO VIEW PARACHURCH MINISTERS AND MINISTRIES

A parachurch ministry is a ministry that operates as a separate entity outside the legal and ecclesial structure of the local church. Many itinerant ministers, great missions organizations, Bible schools, evangelistic associations, some media ministries, college campus outreaches, apologetics ministries, family ministries, prison ministries, and so forth fit this category.

Although I believe God has raised up most of these ministries, I believe Scripture is clear that the local church is the central plan of God (see Eph. 3:9-11) and provides the proper ways and means to properly shepherd the flock of God, process and develop spiritual leadership, and be the leading institution in regard to establishing the Kingdom of God on the earth—community by community.

To be fair to parachurch ministries, oftentimes the local church has not done their part and has become irrelevant in regard to any one of the ministry obligations mentioned above. I believe this is the main reason why God has raised up parachurch ministries. If the Body of Christ in history was faithfully carrying out its ministry obligations, the parachurch ministry probably wouldn't exist, except for those trans-local and extra-local ministries necessary to reflect the needs of the corporate Church in a region.

Unfortunately, the fact that we currently have two different entities attempting to do the same things sometimes leads to friction or competition between the parachurch and the Church. Many pastors have told me they have had bad experiences and don't want to work with parachurch groups anymore.

The problems center on two things: who has the right to minister to the people in the congregations, and who should get the finances. Biblically, the local church has been called to shepherd the sheep (see Heb. 13:7,17; John 21:15-17). The church is also called of God to equip the saints and prepare them for the work of the ministry (see Eph. 4:11-13).

When a traveling minister or ministerial entity outside the local church attempts to equip the saints without cooperating with the leadership of the local church, it causes confusion and divides the loyalties of the sheep away from the spiritual leadership in the church. Parachurch ministries may specialize in certain things, but are not necessarily called of God to speak into your life and process you into maturity.

A parachurch ministry often doesn't have the structure and capacity to minister to the whole family. A church is set up to be "a family of families"; thus, the sheep are tempted to disrespect and ignore the very spiritual leaders appointed by God to nurture them, and in so doing they break the fifth commandment, which results in many unnecessary problems and pains.

I had a situation with one traveling minister in which I politely asked him to check with me before he counseled folks attending our church. He got upset with me and accused me of controlling people. Getting counsel from somebody who doesn't really know you, doesn't live near you, and isn't called of God to do it can cause much confusion. What happens if the leaders of the church say one thing to the person and the parachurch leader says something contrary? Situations like this can disrupt the generational blessings that are supposed to flow into the spiritual sons and daughters in the house of the Lord.

Another reason there is competition between parachurch and local church is finances. Oftentimes traveling ministers want to sign up the folks in our church for a mailing list, and most times I won't let them do it. I know that many of these ministries would hit them up for money every month!

Many radio and television ministers attempt to extract the tithe from their listening audience. Beloved, this should never be! The Bible says in Malachi 3:8-14 to bring the tithe into the storehouse. What is the storehouse? It is where you hold the supply of food so folks can be fed. Being fed is a lot more than hearing a message, a tape, or a television show. The easiest things pastors do is preach on Sunday. Feeding the flock involves holding them accountable, training them, and helping them with their marriages, families, and self-development. It is marrying their children, burying their dead, and visiting their sick. You are not going to get that kind of total care outside of the local church. No wonder God calls it the main entity that will defeat the gates of hell and show to the principalities and powers His divine wisdom! Hallelujah! Folks can pray about giving a portion of their offering to parachurch ministries, but the bulk of their money should come to the storehouse in the local church.

ABOUT JOSEPH MATTERA

JOSEPH Mattera has been in full-time ministry since 1980 and is currently the Presiding Bishop of Christ Covenant Coalition and Overseeing Bishop of Resurrection Church in New York City, a multiethnic congregation of 40 nationalities that has successfully developed numerous leaders and holistic ministry in the New York region and beyond. He is also serving as the United States Ambassador for the International Coalition of Apostles, and as the Third Presiding Bishop of the International Communion of Evangelical Churches.

He has extensively ministered nationally and internationally, reaching out to many nations of the world, including the former Soviet Union, Bulgaria, Turkey, Puerto Rico, the Dominican Republic, Honduras, Holland, the Ukraine, Canada, Mexico, Cuba, Russia, and Argentina, as well as many of the states in the United States. Joseph has a Doctor of Ministry degree in Biblical Worldview from Bakke Graduate University and is the author of three theological books on the Kingdom of God, entitled *Ruling in the Gates* (2003), *Kingdom Revolution* (2009), and *Kingdom Awakening* (2010). He has appeared on nationally known Christian networks such as TBN, Daystar Television Network, and Cornerstone Television Network. He also has numerous original articles, position papers, seminars, sermons, podcasts, and videos presently posted on his Website, www.josephmattera.org.

IN THE RIGHT HANDS, THIS BOOK WILL CHANGE LIVES!

Most of the people who need this message will not be looking for this book. To change their lives, you need to put a copy of this book in their hands.

> *But others (seeds) fell into good ground, and brought forth fruit, some a hundred-fold, some sixty-fold, some thirty-fold* (Matthew 13:8).

Our ministry is constantly seeking methods to find the good ground, the people who need this anointed message to change their lives. Will you help us reach these people?

> *Remember this—a farmer who plants only a few seeds will get a small crop. But the one who plants generously will get a generous crop* (2 Corinthians 9:6).

EXTEND THIS MINISTRY BY SOWING
3 BOOKS, 5 BOOKS, 10 BOOKS, OR MORE TODAY,
AND BECOME A LIFE CHANGER!

Thank you,

Don Nori Sr., Founder
Destiny Image
Since 1982